THE **ESSENTIAL** **ENTREPRENEUR**

THE **ESSENTIAL ENTREPRENEUR**

WHAT IT TAKES TO
START, SCALE AND SELL
A SUCCESSFUL BUSINESS

BY AWARD-WINNING ENTREPRENEUR

RICHARD TURNER

WILEY

First published in 2023 by John Wiley & Sons Australia, Ltd

Level 1, 155 Cremorne St, Richmond Vic 3121

Typeset in Adobe Caslon Pro 11.5pt/15pt

© John Wiley & Sons Australia, Ltd 2023

The moral rights of the author have been asserted

ISBN: 978-1-119-98455-9

A catalogue record for this book is available from the National Library of Australia

Cover design by Wiley
Cover Image: © korkeng / Shutterstock
Author Photo: Peter Fisher Photography

Disclaimer
The material in this publication is of the nature of general comment only, and does not represent professional advice. It is not intended to provide specific guidance for particular circumstances and it should not be relied on as the basis for any decision to take action or not take action on any matter which it covers. Readers should obtain professional advice where appropriate, before making any such decision. To the maximum extent permitted by law, the author and publisher disclaim all responsibility and liability to any person, arising directly or indirectly from any person taking or not taking action based on the information in this publication.

For my family

I would particularly like to dedicate this book to my two greatest mentors: my father, Allan Turner (who passed away in 2006), and my brother and business partner, Greg Turner (who passed away far too soon in 2021).

To my children, Sarah, Laura, James, India and Siena: be inspired as the next generation to protect this planet and make the world a better place for everyone.

And my final dedication, of course, is to my beautiful wife, Sarah Jane, for her unwavering love and support. Darling, I simply could not have done this without you! Xx

CONTENTS

Introduction   *ix*

1   Validating and testing your idea   1

2   Developing a start-up business plan   11

3   Product or service?   27

4   Timing is everything   31

5   Passion, culture and values   39

6   Brand positioning and marketing   49

7   Bringing in those sales   63

8   Sourcing suppliers and manufacturing   73

9   Innovation, re-invention and disruption   83

10 Defining a new market   93

11 Getting investment ready   97

12 Ownership and equity   111

13 Trademarks and patents   125

14 What business am I in?   141

15 Tuning and restructuring   149

16 Managing growth and consistency   155

17 Getting out of business   167

Are entrepreneurs born or made?   *173*

Acknowledgements   *179*

Index   *181*

INTRODUCTION

Starting and running a business can be a most rewarding, but complex and demanding, part of your life. It can give you the independence, lifestyle and financial status you crave, but if it's unsuccessful it can also take away your independence and you are suddenly in damage control trying to protect all that is valuable to you.

It may seem strange to be writing a book on 'the rules' of entrepreneurship, as entrepreneurs, by definition, all do things differently. However, there are fundamentals you need to get right to give yourself the best chance of success when starting a business. Disruption and reinvention are part of those fundamental rules and part of the everyday life of being a successful entrepreneur. This is not a step-by-step 'how to' book, but rather a book of fundamental principles that will be applied differently by different people and different business concepts. But they are fundamentals that must be covered off to give you the best chance of success.

My father always said, 'A good business makes money from day one'—a statement that still carries a lot of merit today. A simple business model that people understand and that works well is often the best, so don't unnecessarily overcomplicate the process. In these days of burning cash before your business plan predicts you will make a profit, and potentially running the risk of your plan failing in the process — leaving large debts behind — keeping it simple is often the best solution.

I was fortunate to have grown up in a business family with my two brothers, and we experienced all that came with that. My father founded what has become one of the largest meat wholesaling and further meat processing businesses in the country.

Every school holidays it was an expectation that I would work at the factory washing walls and cleaning drains to earn some sought-after money. I learned what it took to earn money, and the value of it, and took great satisfaction in saving every week to eventually buy what every teenager in the 1980s wanted: a hi-fi stereo sound system with turntable, amplifier, quality speakers and the latest vinyl records!

In my secondary school years, I was promoted to the production line, packing the offal, and was eventually put in charge of the trimming machine, trimming the meat off the bones that the boners missed with their big knives. At the end of the day the production crew took great joy in throwing me into the boning bin (and I can tell you that's a pretty humbling experience, but it taught me humility, what hard work was about and the real value of money) and as you could imagine the melting pot of cultures that worked in that type of environment was incredibly diverse and taught me a huge amount about how to get on well with virtually anyone I met, an enormously valuable lesson in life.

I was never the brightest kid at school, but I carried that work ethic and humility into the classroom and through sheer determination I managed to scrape into the bottom end of the A-stream classes and then had to continually work hard to stay there. Finding a way (sometimes creatively) to get things done really underpinned the rest of my life as an entrepreneur.

I achieved a high enough score in year 12 to gain entry to the Bachelor of Business degree at the University of South Australia. I was the youngest of three boys but the first to have the opportunity to go to university so I didn't want to waste that gift, and there were expectations of applying what I learned to the family business. It was a time of rapid technological advancement, with our business moving from a Wang computer with a 5" floppy disk that had a simple accounting package to an HP 3000 computer system that took up an entire room. It was specifically climate controlled, with a washing machine-sized CPU, enormous twin 250MB hard drives, reel-to-reel tape drive and twin very loud line printers with ribbons that continually jammed up.

The programming and operation of this system was outsourced to specialists at the time but really took my interest, and learning early BASIC language software coding was part of my degree course. In fact, I was one of the first cohorts to go through the degree to actually learn coding on a keyboard and screen instead of on punch cards. I spent many hours under the guise of my university study sitting with the programmers at the family business as they were defining the core business processes that could be managed by a software program at the time. The initial suite of programs continually needed debugging and I became very good at this and at maintaining and evolving the system until it eventually became my job when I graduated from university in 1984.

This gave the innovator in me the chance to evolve as I loved being the systems analyst and finding any manual task that I could design a program for to automate the process. The big challenge was our livestock trading operation as we needed to track large numbers of cattle purchased, individual live weights and costs, and then the yields after processing, which translated into our true product costs. It was a unique system that was used up to 15 years after I first designed it. It suddenly gave us rapid insight into the most productive buyers, the cattle markets and the cattle breeds that provided the best yields, which in turn provided the business with a significant market advantage. It was my first taste of disrupting an industry to an extent and I remember thinking that was pretty cool at the time.

In 1986 the company went public and, soon after, in 1987, my brothers and I decided to launch into our first business rather than staying with the public entity, preferring to maintain our independence and exploit our industry knowledge and ideas.

This book showcases the key lessons I learned from my four enterprises over the past 35 years across different sectors, together with my more recent work as Entrepreneur in Residence at the University of South Australia and what I call the Fundamental Rules of Successful Entrepreneurship. (I'll use my own businesses, plus a number of others, as working examples where relevant in the chapters of this book.)

As an entrepreneur, you'll make mistakes along the way, and you must learn from those experiences and learn how others have navigated the same issues. In the end you need to simply make more good decisions than bad to survive and be successful. If I can help you avoid some of the fundamental mistakes along the way, I've done my job!

To help me reinforce the points I make in each chapter I have engaged the help of three leading Australian entrepreneurs: Tobi Pearce from SWEAT, Flavia Tata Nardini from Fleet Space Technologies and Simon Haigh from Haigh's Chocolates, together with Kirsten Bernhardt from Artesian Alternative Investments, who will provide an insight into what the leading venture capital funds and investors are looking for in start-up and scale-up companies and founding entrepreneurs.

These inspiring entrepreneurs have incredible stories of how they have built their businesses and will share their own experiences on how they navigated the topics I raise in the chapters of this book. Not every business and business model are the same, but often the underlying problem we are trying to solve is very similar and my experiences, combined with those of the other entrepreneurs, will help you to understand the concepts more thoroughly.

Introducing Tobi Pearce (Ex-CEO and Co-founder of SWEAT)

Tobi and co-founder Kayla Itsines built a global online fitness empire that started in 2015 with their local personal training group, turning their workout routines into a product that could be targeted to an audience and distributed globally. Tobi and Kayla completed a deal with iFIT in July 2021, selling SWEAT for a reported $400 million. The company had an annual revenue of $100 million, reaching a global community of more than 50 million women across its social media channels to help them reach their fitness goals. The app is translated into eight languages and available in 155 countries.

Tobi grew up in a small town located near the wine region of McLaren Vale just south of Adelaide in South Australia. He admits there was no degree of entrepreneurship in or around his family, and business was never really spoken about when he was a child. Business and money were only really discussed in the context that 'we didn't have heaps', and life was typical and frugal for Tobi while growing up. Tobi's father was passionate about wine. He worked in a local winey, both in the vineyard and doing tastings, and started a small winery tour business, working for himself. It was never really talked about as a business or even a job: it just worked for his lifestyle and was never designed to be a commercial venture.

Tobi was an avid reader and read more books than most when he was younger, although certainly not business books at the time. However, he just knew from the knowledge he gained he wanted more from life. He didn't know what he wanted, but he knew he wanted to be successful. From an upbringing of being financially limited, he knew he had to budget and save to get the things he wanted and by eight or nine years of age he started doing the maths on how long it would take him to save for his first TV.

Tobi left home at a young age while still at school and had a practical problem to solve: he needed a place to live and sleep and food to eat, all of which required money. He ended up having a few different jobs to pay his way, moving back in and out of home over that time, and eventually, after completing school, he thought, *now what?* Even though year 12 wasn't Tobi's best year at school, he decided he wanted to go to university with the aspiration of getting into business, so with sheer determination he decided to sit a mature-age entry exam. Tobi needed to study hard to get the required score, and he achieved enough points to embark on a double degree of Commerce and Law at Flinders University.

He made it through nearly four of the six-year double degree but found it difficult to earn income and study full time, and to complete the course part time would have taken far too long (another six years). As opportunity would have it, for two years prior Tobi had been going to the gym to lift weights as part of a recovery program for a back injury. He admits to being a skinny—but athletic—kid and enjoyed the gym experience.

His journey from this point is remarkable, and you will learn about how the SWEAT business evolved in the chapters ahead.

Introducing Flavia Tata Nardini (CEO and Co-founder of Fleet Space Technologies)

Flavia Tata Nardini and co-founder Matt Pearson have built a globally leading 'space technology' business literally from their garage over the past few years, bringing their idea of building small communications satellites to life. The business is changing the economics of space communications, enabling many new industry applications. Fleet made history by launching Australia's first four commercial nanosatellites in November 2018. Over the course of three weeks, Proxima 1 and 2 and Centauri 1 and 2 were launched into low Earth orbit. Fleet is continuing its work on the Centauri program, having launched its fifth and sixth satellites in 2021, and the next batch of satellites in 2022.

Flavia is a native of Italy and grew up in a family of five siblings, a family who were all high achieving engineers across different disciplines. Her grandfather had three degrees in engineering, and engineering, in various forms, was always a topic of conversation in her family—but no-one had ever done space!

Flavia admits she was born with a love for space, more so than engineering, that she can't really explain. She was obsessed with the stars from a very young age and a huge fan of space movies, which she admits most young children are—but Flavia never moved on! Her obsession with space continued throughout high school and took different forms. She first wanted to be an astronaut, then an astronomer, then she wanted to find extra-terrestrial life and then she became fascinated with stars as her interest became more sophisticated. Flavia was good with maths at school and with her family being engineers she decided to pursue becoming a space engineer.

Flavia had always worked in larger corporations and had no experience with start-ups. She openly admits that start-ups were not her thing; none of her family members had done a start-up before. When she moved to Australia, she couldn't find a job in the space industry as it just 'wasn't a thing' in Australia at the time. However, she wanted to keep working in space. In Australia, as a matter of chance, she met co-founder Matt Pearson, who is a true entrepreneur at heart and, as Flavia says, 'It is his thing!' For Matt, start-ups were his way of living and he had been founding start-ups since his twenties, including a very successful software start-up in Sydney with up to 300 employees, so when they met it was a match made in space! As a typical 'no fear' young entrepreneur Matt said, 'If I can do software, I can do space!'

Together with Flavia's technical skills and leading the business as CEO, they are building an inspirational business to 'enable the next giant leap in human civilisation'. From humble beginnings you'll learn how this business started and evolved chapter by chapter in the book.

Introducing Simon Haigh (Joint Managing Director of Haigh's Chocolates)

Simon and his brother Alister are the fourth generation of this extraordinary 107-year-old iconic business, which has produced four generations of exceptional entrepreneurs. As Australia's oldest family-owned chocolate maker, they have not only had to validate the idea, and establish and grow the business and the brand, but also to continually adapt and transition the business in a rapidly changing world over more than a century. You will hear how the original business was founded by Simon's great grandfather, Alfred E Haigh, in 1915, and how every generation of the Haigh family has tackled a different level of entrepreneurship with its own unique challenges as the company has matured and grown.

Haigh's has built a brand and product over 107 years that is close to the heart of many Australians and continues to expand nationally with its ever-growing retail and manufacturing operations—and is now even considering international markets. Every stage is like starting a new business in a new era, and as timing is everything in entrepreneurship, this requires the same process and entrepreneurial thinking every time. It's an incredible view of a multi-generational business staying relevant and maintaining market leadership over time.

Simon grew up in Adelaide but did his school years with brother Alister boarding at Geelong Grammar in Victoria, coming home during holidays in the mid 1960s to work in the business to earn some much-needed money at the time. Simon describes the work as more 'running riot in the factory' and 'handing out chocolates to shoppers'.

The business was still a real family affair at the time, with their mother heavily involved in designing and preparing the packaging for the Easter range and how it would all come together and be displayed.

Neither Alister nor Simon went straight into the business after school. Alister did some jackerooing up north in South Australia and both spent time in Masterton, New Zealand, at a family friend's horse stud 'Te Parae' learning the trade. As you will hear in the story of the earlier generations, horse studs were a big part of the Haigh's business interests, and during some tough times around the Great Depression played a strong part in supporting the chocolate business. Simon had aspirations of becoming a vet but getting into veterinary science at the time was very difficult, with only one or two colleges available in Australia. Both came back from New Zealand and after a reality check started working in the business, learning the operational side. The company had a strong operational and retail team, and working under their father, John Haigh, provided Alister and Simon with the best learning platform possible.

Simon talks about each generation of the Haigh family and how they navigated their entrepreneurial challenges in the following chapters.

Introducing Kirsten Bernhardt (Investment Manager at Artesian Alternative Investments)

Kirsten Bernhardt joined Artesian Alternative Investments in 2022 as Investment Manager of the South Australian Venture Capital Fund. Kirsten spent two years in San Francisco, where she was Investment Strategist with legal software and law firm start-up Atrium before moving to Bank of America as Assistant Vice President, Middle Market Technology Banking. She was Commercial Manager with The University of Adelaide and a consultant with both Ernst & Young and KPMG prior to her move overseas.

Her new role with Artesian—the global venture capital fund managers responsible for the $50 million South Australian Venture Capital Fund as part of their portfolio—will see her focused on investing capital into South Australian tech start-ups.

Not all businesses want to raise money and have investment partners; many will self-fund their own development from their savings (known as 'bootstrapping') and others will fund through the business earnings (though not everyone has that option). If the market opportunity is only available for a small window of time, or you simply don't have the financial resources to get started, then you will need other partners or investors to join you on the journey. In this instance, you need to ask yourself, *Do you need skills* and *money or just the money?* This is a fundamental question when you're starting out.

Kirsten provides us with tremendous insight on how investors look at founding entrepreneurs and their businesses, what they consider to be investible businesses and why. This is absolutely critical information to understand when you're starting a business that you want to scale quickly and you need investors to help finance that journey. Understanding how to present not only yourself, but also your team, the business and the right business model from early on and understanding what investors are looking for will get you financed and underway much faster to grow your dream.

* * *

Now that you've been personally introduced to my panel, look out for their invaluable advice and insights throughout the book. Each chapter that is relevant to some aspect of Tobi's, Flavia's, Simon's or Kirsten's expertise will include information on their experience to help reinforce the chapter's focus.

I can't wait to share this content with you and to hear your success stories later! Validating your idea and testing the market is a great place to start—so let's get cracking!

CHAPTER 1

Validating and testing your idea

We've all stood around the BBQ with family and friends having a drink and solving the world's problems, or at least coming up with lots of ideas on how things could be done better. How many of those ideas actually turn into something the next day? Realistically, almost none!

So, what if you put your money where your mouth is and give it a go? Where would you start to conceive how it could work? Did everyone agree it was a great idea? Is the timing right and would they pay for your product or service if it was available, and how much would they pay?

Is the idea novel (has it been done before) or are you just trying to improve on what's already in the market? Is the idea scalable or is it limited to just being a small business? What are the barriers to turning it from a small business into a large or even global business? You may be content with just a small business, or you may be ambitious and want to build a global business, so it's critical to consider how you would scale if that's your goal.

If you really felt inspired by people's reactions to your idea, then get online and start researching to find out whether anything like it exists, and if it does, how similar is it to your idea, and what makes your idea so much better?

Then test the idea out with other groups of friends to further validate and refine your thinking: you might even uncover some potential business partners. This initial 'market research' phase is critically important for understanding the potential opportunity. We'll go into the validation process in more detail throughout the book.

If it is a product or a service to industry rather than direct to consumers, you need to follow the same validation process, but before you talk with potential customers or partners it's crucial to protect your idea so that no-one else can easily steal it. This can be done in the first instance by writing up a non-disclosure agreement (NDA), which is a standard document with a tailored purpose that a general solicitor can provide you with quickly for a relatively low cost. You need to talk with businesses in your target market and thoroughly test your idea. Then, if you feel really inspired and compelled to take it a step further, it's time to get cracking on a simple business plan (which I'll run you through in detail in chapter 2) to thoroughly test your thinking.

Most businesses fail in the transition from an idea to actually creating and running a real business, which requires a very different skillset, and you need to be well prepared for the journey ahead, which comes down to planning.

Let's take a look at how my panel navigated this tricky step.

Tobi's start-up story

While he was studying at university, Tobi met a personal trainer at the gym where he was training who has since become a lifelong mate. He told Tobi that while he was studying at university, he worked as a personal trainer (PT) on the side. He was making $70 to $90 per hour and could book clients around his own schedule. At the time, Tobi was earning around $15 per hour doing various jobs, so he thought that was 'unbelievable!' He already enjoyed fitness and had just done some fitness competitions, and he saw this as an 'awesome' opportunity, so he started the process of getting his PT qualification.

Tobi quickly dropped his other jobs and started focusing on personal training. He had to earn $400 to $500 per week to cover his living costs, which he quickly calculated he could do in significantly fewer hours than he had been working.

With a PT qualification under his belt, Tobi soon had clients of his own, and he quickly became obsessed with growing his business for both the financial and learning opportunities it could offer. He focused on being as successful as possible and soon realised he was learning more in this practical business setting than he was learning at university.

Tobi earned around $100000 in his first year as a personal trainer, and then had the realisation in his second year that he could do small group sessions and earn more per hour while working fewer hours. He was very focused on observation and learning, and understanding his clientele and their attitudes. Most of his clients were female and in two age groups, being around 19–20 or 35–40. Within that range, there appeared to be several different key attitudes or behaviours: with or without kids was a big divider for understanding the audience and the preferences of their individual fitness journeys.

His next thought was that he could do even bigger groups if he went outdoors, increasing his earnings to between $250000 to $500000 over the next couple of years. He continued to grow while maintaining very positive feedback. With too many clients to look after on his own, Tobi got other people to help with the sessions. Clients also wanted to do work outside of the sessions, which begged the question: *How do I make income from that?* 'Books' was the idea: *I'll write some eBooks that I can sell to my clients!*

Collaborating with some dietitians, he started with a book on nutrition advice, which he admits was a minimum viable product (MVP) but at the time it did okay. This was launched in November 2013. At the same time, he was putting a lot of effort into creating workout programs and custom programs, which were released in January 2014 as the photography involved delayed them coming out together as the one book initially. Tobi says they served their purpose, taking his earnings to around $500000 per year.

(continued)

In breaking down the income, he realised about 80 per cent was coming from bootcamps and personal training so there was still a lot of scope to increase the programming income. He had recently met partner and SWEAT co-founder Kayla and they had started posting programs on social media. In Tobi's words, 'we were killing it' (compared to anything else that was around at the time). While acknowledging that social media was in its infancy at that time, and not yet fully integrated with the world the way it is today, they saw an opportunity and considered this as a way of selling legitimate eBooks online instead of only existing customers ordering them.

They saw a gap in the market for programs that met the psychological and attitudinal profile of their young female market, highlighting confidence and empowerment over aesthetics effectively. It was a combination of the right product with the right audience at the right time. What Tobi had learned at university he was now able to apply in his own business.

Validating the SWEAT business

Tobi was confident there was an unmet business need as clients were looking for something outside of their bootcamp sessions, so he needed to understand what the customer actually wanted. What could the business provide that met the need: where was the middle ground? Tobi had a deep understanding of his clientele after thousands of PT sessions. He spent more time in the gym than any other trainer there, sometimes just sitting around watching people, not even running sessions but just observing behaviours. What do they wear? How do they train? What are their goals? When do they train? What's their motivation to train?

From this understanding he started to put the product out. Before the eBooks were digitised and scaled, they were originally done on a one-on-one basis with clients. When he caught up with his clients, he would also be doing a Q&A session on the personalised book, asking 'How are you feeling? What do and don't you understand? Is it too advanced? Can you progress with it or are you regressing?' It was fundamental physiology and frameworks. Over time there was an understanding of the sensitivities. Tobi says, 'There was too much of this and not enough of that', so they would tweak things for people as needed, which, Tobi learned during the process, was actually a way of achieving product-market fit.

Once the book was digitised, both the product and the support became more sophisticated and Tobi would spend time on the help desk understanding the questions — the frequency of certain questions — that were being asked by email. The beauty of an eBook is that it's relatively low cost to modify, so repeating themes could quickly and easily be addressed, and the eBook updated. 'We'll reword this, or write a new chapter on that, or delete this ...' was effectively the process. At this point Tobi considered himself an apprentice of the game, looking at, listening to and observing everything, looking for ways to improve. He would read all the social media comments and emails every week (sometimes up to 10 000) including any media publications they were featured in and every associated comment that was made. He would try to read absolutely everything to understand how the books were being perceived, how the brand was being perceived and how the product was being perceived. Tobi and Kayla became very customer directed in their development as a business through a natural evolution.

Flavia's start-up story

Flavia was working with small satellites, with dreams of these satellites solving major challenges for our civilisation both now and into the future. But it was in effect technology looking for a problem and was very much driven by Flavia and Matt's combined passion. The trend was towards small satellites and the economics were stacking up to get them into space — but for what?

Flavia and Matt founded a start-up before Fleet Space that was building small satellites for schools. It was basically launching a GoPro into space for school kids to take photos of Earth, which Flavia says, 'was pretty damn cool!' It was fun and made enough money to allow them to take time to go and talk to people and industry to try to find an application for her satellites.

(continued)

Flavia spent a couple of years in coffee shops (averaging 10 coffees a week — a lot for someone who doesn't drink coffee!) talking to people who were potential users of satellites. This was to understand what the thing was that people needed space technology for. 'I want to build satellites; do you have any problems that we can solve with this technology?' During this process, Flavia realised the problems that could be solved from space fell largely into two buckets: people who needed connectivity around the world (people without internet) and industrial connectivity for businesses with machinery or infrastructure in remote areas.

Elon Musk's SpaceX was already tackling the first problem. Should they go up against SpaceX? Their thinking was 'no!' It was a huge problem with a lot of complexity that a multi-billionaire was already trying to solve. On the other hand, connectivity for industrial applications was very much unserved, spanning through sectors including agriculture, mining and energy. 'We like this bucket; its achievable — let's jump on it.'

Within a year they had started the company with a concept utilising space to advance industrial 'Internet of Things' (IoT) applications. They needed to get test applications underway and Matt was great at building software, but it would take one and a half years to build a satellite, which was too long. So, they decided to use an available satellite company even though it was pricey, over dimensioned and 'a pain too'. But it allowed them to be operational in the field. With the initial applications they knew this set-up was a recipe for disaster because of the costs. However, they also knew they could dramatically reduce the operating costs with their own satellites in time. They set up the initial test applications to pilot at a low price, knowing they would lose money, but at least they were in the field operating and finding the right applications to build their own network for.

Validating the Fleet Space Technologies business

The first test was with technology geeks of the various target sectors: influential industry people who really liked tech — farmers who liked tech; mining and energy people who liked tech — so they could get feedback about the product. Flavia openly admits up to 90 per cent of their first efforts were terrible and they were embarrassed by them, but they were given an enormous amount of feedback on the test applications.

There were geeky farmers who were looking to monitor their cows, soil and tanks, and energy companies monitoring solar farms. Using satellites for this didn't make sense, though, because satellites cost thousands per month whereas cows only cost hundreds, but they did receive useful, in-depth analyses about what was affordable and what wasn't. Basically, the result was: 'It would be good to monitor the soil and have that information, but who really cares'. From this research they were able to start culling applications that were not economical and people who were unlikely to pay. In a good year it may have been affordable for farmers, but in a crisis, it wouldn't have been, and they would simply revert to getting in a car to check on their cows.

Flavia and Matt needed an application that would be a game changer for the industry. In year three (2020) — at the beginning of the COVID-19 pandemic — they eliminated all the 'nice to have' applications and lined up four target applications: hydro (water monitoring), gas (pipeline monitoring), electricity (transmission and distribution monitoring) and mining (exploration). If satellites could monitor a pipeline or a transformer, instead of having to use people, there's a significant efficiency gain. The application needed to produce a saving in the millions of dollars per year, not just a couple of cows!

For two years they worked in these four sectors, recognising that for a start-up it was very important to focus so they didn't spread their resources too thinly. Covering these markets was a lot of work, and it was important to identify the applications that would save their customers a lot of money and that weren't just a 'nice to have'.

Preventing blackouts at an electricity distribution business (electricity poles and wires), for instance, was a key priority. Informing a client that a transformer was overheating or exploding when there was no-one supervising it could save them $500 000 to $1 million per year, so they were happy to spend a few thousand dollars per year on the solution.

Despite these being useful and efficient applications, they were really just a 'side gig' in terms of income for the business. This wasn't going to be the game changer Flavia and Matt were after. They needed much more than this to create a large, sustainable and growing business.

(continued)

Unfortunately, this wasn't a way to avoid blackouts, and only created a more efficient monitoring process.

Three out of the four applications they had been working on for the previous couple of years turned out to be a good side income but not the game changer they were looking for.

But one showed potential, as we'll see in later chapters ...

Haigh's Chocolates' start-up story

Alf Haigh (as he was affectionately known by the family) was born in 1877, raised in Adelaide and then moved to Jamestown in South Australia's mid north in 1884 with his family, where he opened a confectionery store in 1896 at 19 years of age. In this era the store would have sold primarily boiled sweets and lollies. Alf got married and moved to Fremantle in Western Australia to try his hand at mining gold during the gold rush of the 1890s, but returned to Jamestown six months later to work for a supplier of agricultural bindings and equipment. It was there that he developed a piece of technology and had his first patent registered. The entrepreneurial brain was already working!

In 1905 Alf moved to Mt Gambier in South Australia, where his entrepreneurial legacy really commenced when he opened a fruit and confectionery business together with a cool drinks factory and introduced ice-cream into his range in 1909. Not to be underdone, Alf also became manager of the Imperial Picture Company, running silent movies at the local Institute Hall. He then opened two more stores in regional South Australia before moving back to Adelaide in 1913 where he opened a further two suburban stores.

In 1915 Alf purchased a confectionery business operating in Adelaide from a European-trained confectioner, Carl Stratmann. With World War I spreading anti-German sentiment, Carl's business was struggling, so he agreed to sell it to Alf — including all equipment, stock, recipes and the trademark 'Confiserie Surfine', which still appears on Haigh's Chocolates packaging today. The business was located in the famous

Beehive Corner building in the Adelaide CBD where Haigh's flagship retail store remains to this day.

Alf was enthusiastic about the chocolate business, as well as property development, and he opened a factory on Greenhill Road in Adelaide in 1922 that is also still in operation today. He sold the Mt Gambier businesses and started making chocolate at the new factory using beans from Ghana, Venezuela, Trinidad and Ecuador. He built shops and houses along the Adelaide foreshore at Henley Beach, including the well-known Haigh Mansions, and ran a footwear store. He also built a five-storey building with basements in Rundle Street known as the 'Haigh's building' where he opened cafés in the basements.

Recognising the annual opportunity to sell more chocolate, Haigh's started making chocolate Easter eggs and penny chocolate frogs, and as a result Alf extended the Haigh's factory to cope with the added demand at the time, even hand-making boxes at the factory. He then acquired the rights to sell confectionery at the Adelaide Oval, which Haigh's continued doing for about 50 years. Alf also opened numerous stores and purchased an 860-acre property at Mallala for his horse breeding interests.

He was a 'true entrepreneur,' and as Simon describes him, a 'Jack of all trades', having the opportunistic foresight and ability to successfully start, grow and trade various business interests. Alf died suddenly in 1933 at age 55 which, on reflection, says Simon, 'may have been fortuitous for the longevity of the Haigh's Chocolate business' as, being the constant trader that Alf was, it could easily have been sold in any of his ongoing business dealings. For the millions of Haigh's Chocolate fans around the world today this would be a very uncomfortable thought to process!

Validating the Haigh's Chocolate business

Alf's son Claude took over the business in 1933 at age 30 after Alf passed away. He grew up in Mt Gambier and moved to Adelaide with his family, where he completed high school. Claude was trained as a bookkeeper and worked for a shipping agent at the time.

Being a bookkeeper, Claude had the skills to stabilise and consolidate the business, applying a 'methodical mind and steady hand' essential for

(continued)

the management of the various business interests, including the retail and manufacturing operations. He never really worked in the factory or the practical side of the business, leaving that to the exceptional experience of Harold Lewis, who started with Alf in 1912 and who knew the operational side of the chocolate business inside and out.

Claude's focus was his six thoroughbred fillies: this marked the beginning of the family's Balcrest Stud, which developed as the other side of the family business. Balcrest Stud was the foremost stud in South Australia for many years with the importation of the leading brood mare sire Coronation Boy. Claude sold the Mallala property in 1934 and relocated the stud to a new location at Balhannah in the Adelaide Hills, where the property remains today. At one stage, Balcrest took home 75 per cent of the proceeds of the South Australian yearling sales!

During the Great Depression, Haigh's Chocolates settled into a period of quiet stability which continued into the 1940s, opening only two stores during that period. There were times during those years when the horses supported the chocolate business — until the tides turned and the chocolate business began supporting the horses.

Claude bought the Beehive Corner building that became part of the family's property business. Claude's health, however, was steadily failing, so his son John had to enter the business from a young age. John's entry marked the beginning of a period of remarkable innovation and progression for the Haigh's Chocolate business as we'll discover later in the book.

Essentially...

- Is the timing right? (You'll read much more about this in chapter 4.)
- You must validate your business idea before you start spending money.
- Are there customers who will pay for your idea?
- How much would they be willing to pay?

CHAPTER 2

Developing a start-up business plan

It's quite astonishing to me just how many people can't clearly articulate their business model and how and why it will be a success. Why is it a good idea? Is there a customer who will pay for your product? How have you validated that? How big is the market? Who is your competition and what's your point of difference? How many units do you have to sell, and at what price and margin, to be profitable? Who are your potential customers and how will you communicate with them? How much money do you need? These are confronting questions, but if you're going to have the best chance of success they need to be answered.

Developing a start-up business plan is absolutely fundamental to success. If you're bringing partners on board, either for their skills or financial support, you must be able to clearly articulate and demonstrate what the opportunity is and how the business will be profitable.

In chapter 11, I'll present a great business presentation format for all potential stakeholders, not just investors. Then, in chapters 12 to 17, I'll detail the important business aspects that will feed into your business plan. But first, in this chapter, we're going to look at the key information that every plan must contain.

Market validation

After talking to family and friends about your business idea, the next step is to approach potential real customers and suppliers to validate your model. This is an *essential* step (because chances are your family and friends are just being nice to you). Testing the model in the real commercial world will give you the hard answers before you invest your valuable time and money. Is the timing right and what would customers be prepared to pay? Are there manufacturers or suppliers who could manufacture the product and at what cost, factoring in freight, import duties and taxes if it's coming from overseas? Does this allow enough margin to make a profit that would cover your operating and marketing costs, and pay the salaries?

Before you talk to potential commercial partners, you might want to consider protecting your idea by having a non-disclosure agreement (NDA) drafted up by a solicitor (you'll recall we discussed NDAs in chapter 1). This is a standard document and should be relatively inexpensive to prepare. It will give you some peace of mind, but be aware that NDAs are more a deterrent than ultimate protection because they can be challenged. Once your idea is out there and you have strong validation, you need to move quickly to protect it. At some point early on, you may decide to register a provisional patent on the product, technology or process (chapter 13 will give you more information on this). To find out if a potential business name is available you will need to search your Government's business name register. In Australia use the Australian Securities and Investments Commission (ASIC) website to conduct this search. After this you will also need to register the web domain and relevant social media pages — and even a trademark on keywords within the proposed business name if you deem this necessary to protect yourself from a branding perspective.

Revenue and profit

At this point, if you're serious about moving forward, I would start looking for an accountant and/or mentor who can be a sounding board to test your business model and ideas. Finding the right accountant can take a bit of time and research. I suggest looking for a smaller, personable accounting firm with an accountant who specialises in start-ups. Talk to a few until you find someone who is enthusiastic about what you're doing, and who you're very comfortable with on a personal level. The right accountant knows they have to be cost effective for start-ups to use, and that money will be tight initially. The right accountant will also have a longer term view to building a valuable future customer and a long-term strategic relationship. As you grow and reach the stage of forming your first board, your accountant will often be one of the first people you ask to be on your board.

If you have no basic accounting experience, I would strongly recommend you do a short accounting course to learn the basics. This will help you understand the principles involved in planning a successful business. Being able to read and understand a simple profit-and-loss statement, balance sheet and cash-flow statement is essential to successfully managing a business at all levels, particularly during the volatile early stages of start-up and scale-up (growth).

The revenue model should show clearly how many units of your product or service you predict to sell each year over the first three years as well as the revenue dollars and profit attached to this. Sales should be broken down by product and customer type to indicate a clear understanding of why you believe you'll sell these quantities (your go-to-market plan) and how you'll reach your customer. The first year is the main focus at this stage, and the one you'll have most clarity about. The second and third years are purely forecasts designed to get you thinking about what could be achieved and how.

Go-to-market plan and operations

Your operating model indicates how you're going to make your idea happen. It should demonstrate a clear understanding of what makes your product or service unique in the market. Will you market and sell it directly to your clients (online and/or through retail outlets) or will you distribute it through reseller/wholesale distribution channels? If you choose the latter, be sure to include an allowance for your resellers by building in substantially more profit—and remember to consider the cost of marketing for them too. How are you going to overcome market barriers to entry: will this require physical warehousing and logistics? What staff, processes and governance are involved? Who is your competition and who could become competition by tweaking their existing business?

All operational details should be described here so that you or a potential investor have a clear understanding of how the business will operate and are convinced of its chances of success. You're sure to be surprised at how this process helps to clarify your own thinking about how you'll operate and achieve success.

Cost validation

What will your costs be to run the operating model so that you're confident of making a profit and, more importantly, a return on your investment that's appropriate for the risk you're taking?

There are three key financial reports that you must be across when running a business: the profit-and-loss statement, the balance sheet and the cash-flow statement. In your model, it's best to break down the operating costs, as you would in a profit-and-loss statement, by showing your top-line revenue (sales) and then deducting your direct cost of goods sold (stock purchases) to come up with your gross profit. You then deduct your operating expenses (all the detailed operating, logistics and administration costs, and wages), giving you your net profit (before tax). Some costs are variable: that is, they will change depending on the amount of product you produce or deliver; delivery costs may be an example of this. Other costs, such as rent, are fixed; that is, they don't change. Costs are usually separated into the categories 'variable' and 'fixed' in your profit-and-loss statement. Allowing for costs that are due at certain times of the year—including insurances, licences, subscriptions and taxes—is important when planning. These costs should be entered in your cash-flow statement so you can see clearly when they are payable and the impact they may have on your available cash at the time. See figure 2.1 for an example profit-and-loss statement.

Profit-and-loss statement for the year ended 30 June 20XX		
	$	$
	20XX	20XX
INCOME		
Sales		
LESS: COST OF GOODS SOLD		
Less: opening stock		
Purchases		
Add: closing stock		
	0	0
GROSS PROFIT	0	0
Gross profit percentage	%	%
ADD: OTHER INCOME		
Interest income		
Sundry income		
	0	0
LESS: FIXED OVERHEADS		
Accounting fees		
Advertising		
Bank fees		
Internet		
Light and power		
Rent		
Sundry		

Figure 2.1: example of a profit-and-loss statement (*continued overleaf*)

Superannuation		
Telephone		
Wages		
	0	0
NET PROFIT (EBITDA: Earnings Before Interest, Tax, Depreciation and Amortisation)	**0**	**0**
LESS:		
Depreciation		
Amortisation		
Interest paid		
	0	0
NET PROFIT (EBT: Earnings Before Tax)	**0**	**0**
LESS:		
Income tax		
NET PROFIT AFTER TAX	**0**	**0**

Figure 2.1: example of a profit-and-loss statement (*cont'd*)

The balance sheet displays the company's total assets and how the assets are financed, either through debt (borrowed funds) or equity (retained profits or owner contributions). There are three key measures in a balance sheet: assets, liabilities and remaining equity (being the assets less the liabilities).

Assets are a combination of things you own and those that have value in your business and they include physical items such as buildings, plant and equipment, and vehicles. They also include cash in the bank and money owed to your business. These are split into 'current assets', being items that can be quickly converted to cash to meet liabilities due in the short term—such as cash in the bank or money owed to you—and 'non-current assets', being the remaining items that can't be turned into cash quickly.

Liabilities include current liabilities such as cash owed to suppliers, banks and others in the short term. Non-current liabilities include anything that doesn't have to be repaid in the short term, such as long-term finance.

Equity is the fundamental measure of the health of your business because it's the remaining value a business has after liabilities are deducted.

So:

$$Assets - liabilities = equity$$

which is the business's value and includes any contributions and retained earnings from previous years. If this goes into a negative balance — meaning you have negative value in the business, and your liabilities exceed your assets — you most likely won't be able to meet your liabilities when they are due, and as a result you're technically trading 'insolvent' and are required by law to wind up your business.

The real focus is on your *current assets* less your *current liabilities*. This is deemed the 'acid test' and it clearly indicates if you'll be unable to meet your payments when they're due. Of course, this can be quickly resolved by putting more money into the business, but you'll have to decide whether the business is viable to continue and whether the problem is a temporary issue that will be overcome. You don't want to be throwing good money after bad. See figure 2.2 for an example balance sheet.

Balance sheet for the year ended 30 June 20XX		
	$	$
ASSETS	20XX	20XX
CURRENT ASSETS		
Cash		
Accounts receivable		
Inventory		
Other current assets		

Figure 2.2: example of a balance sheet (*continued overleaf*)

TOTAL CURRENT ASSETS	0	0
NON-CURRENT (FIXED) ASSETS		
Property, plant and equipment		
Less: accumulated depreciation		
Goodwill		
Other fixed assets		
TOTAL NON-CURRENT (FIXED) ASSETS	0	0
TOTAL ASSETS	0	0
LIABILITIES		
CURRENT LIABILITIES		
Accounts payable		
Credit cards		
Provision for income tax		
Other current liabilities		
TOTAL CURRENT LIABILITIES	0	0
NON-CURRENT (LONG-TERM) LIABILITIES		
Other long-term liabilities		
TOTAL NON-CURRENT (LONG-TERM) LIABILITIES	0	0
TOTAL LIABILITIES	0	0
NET ASSETS / (LIABILITIES)	0	0
EQUITY		
Equity capital/settled sum		
Retained earnings		
TOTAL EQUITY	0	0

Figure 2.2: example of a balance sheet (*cont'd*)

The cash-flow statement (see figure 2.3 for an example) is designed to help you manage and provide for future cash requirements in the short and long term. It shows cash coming in, usually by month, and liabilities for cash going out so you can better manage the business operations to ensure the money is available when payments (current liabilities) are due.

Cash flow statement for the year ended 30 June 20XX		
	$	$
	20XX	20XX
Cash at the beginning of the year		
Cash at the end of the year		
OPERATING ACTIVITIES		
Cash receipts from		
Customers		
Other operations		
Cash paid for		
Inventory purchases		
General operating/admin expenses		
Wage expenses		
Interest		
Income tax		
Other cash items from operation activities		
Net cash flow from operations		
INVESTING ACTIVITIES		
Cash receipts from		
Sale of property and equipment		
Collection of principal on loans		
Sale of investment securities		
Other cash items from investing activities		

Figure 2.3: example of a cash-flow statement (*continued overleaf*)

Cash paid for		
Purchase of property and equipment		
Making loans to other entities		
Purchase of investment securities		
Other cash items from investing activities		
Net cash flow from investment activities	0	0
FINANCING ACTIVITIES		
Cash receipts from		
Issuance of stock		
Borrowing		
Other cash items from financing activities		
Cash paid for		
Repayment of loans		
Dividends		
Other cash items from financing activities		
Net cash flow from financing activities		
NET CASH FLOWS		
CASH AND CASH EQUIVALENTS		
Cash and cash equivalents at beginning of period		
Net change in cash for the period		
Cash and cash equivalents at end of period		
Cash at end of period		

Figure 2.3: example of a cash-flow statement (*cont'd*)

Profitability

What profit margin are you going to make on your product or service (that is, the gross margin as a percentage and the gross margin as a dollar value) so you're confident of covering the operating costs with an appropriate profit still remaining (the net profit)?

Acceptable returns will vary between industries and sectors—whether they're retail or wholesale—and are usually related to trading volumes and business maturity. However, as a rule of thumb for a start-up or a scale-up business, a minimum 10 per cent net profit before tax after all costs are deducted is a good guide for most trading businesses in today's market. A technology business, however, may target a 70 per cent + net profit because its ongoing costs are often quite low once the software is developed and operational. Costs are based more on software updates and improvements, as well as providing support.

Funding

How are you going to fund your business? Can the business be based on a self-funding model early on or will you need significant capital to get started? Will it be self-funding using its own profits after that? Are you putting in the initial money or will it be shared across a number of founders (this is known as 'bootstrapping')? The most common source of initial funds for a start-up come from what's known as the 'three Fs': family, friends and fools. These will often be your first investors: those who want to support you to give your idea a go. Banks are unlikely to lend money against an idea because it's generally risky if there's no proven track record or guarantee you can pay the money back (unless you have some assets you can borrow against, in which case you take all the risk). Check to see if there are any grants available that you could apply for to assist you in getting started. Or you might find investors who can bring both money and additional skills to the table. We'll talk more about this in chapters 11 and 12.

A business start-up grant in a particular industry sector you're looking to enter, if you're lucky enough to qualify, can be very useful. But before you get too excited, be aware that not all grants are 100 per cent free money. Many require a contribution from the founders so that there's some skin in the game, which ensures a much higher commitment to success. You'll find that many grants are 1:1, meaning you'll be up for an equal contribution. Some are 1:2 or even 1:3, which are better odds for you as they provide a greater leverage of your money. If you succeed in getting your business through to a rapid growth phase and consider venture capital (VC) money later on, the VC funders will also look for private investment to match or leverage against, because part of their due-diligence process is to ensure others besides the VC fund are confident your business has what it takes to be successful.

Creating a three-year forecast

As we've seen, to set yourself up for success it's a good idea to create a simple profit-and-loss statement for the first three years of your proposed business. Hiring an accountant who has experience with start-up business models, and who can help you review those financial models and assist you in preparing a plan that potential investors or partners can clearly understand, will help give others confidence in your business concept and capability. The plan should allow for the following expected and unexpected scenarios:

- performing above expectations

- performing at expectation

- breaking even

- failure.

Starting a business is an exercise that will consume a large portion of your life and cause a great deal of stress, so you need to feel you'll be suitably rewarded. There's no point in starting a business if the profit you're going to make gives you the same return as putting your money in the bank (or other safe haven)—you might as well go surfing instead.

Once you have a plan in place, you *must* go over it time and time *and* time again with an accountant or a mentor who has experience in supporting or starting a new business, until everyone is confident that this business is ready for action. Successful business people are often willing to give back by helping others who are starting out, so look for an expert in the field you're considering and don't be afraid to invite them out for a coffee and ask them some questions about your new business concept. Most universities in major cities have a business incubator with access to mentors and they often have positions available in start-up programs, so that might be a place to start.

An experienced mentor will be able to quickly test a model and ask the hard questions related to market reality and readiness as well as how to support and justify the numbers used in the model. This is not to put you down, be difficult or make your life hard—it's to ensure you don't lose everything in the process by making fundamental mistakes that could have been avoided through careful planning. Starting a business isn't easy; if it were, everyone would be doing it and succeeding. Unfortunately, the vast majority fail and it's usually due to poor planning and/or poor execution.

Setting yourself up

Once you and your accountant agree that you have a sound and workable business concept, they will be able to help you with advice on setting up a business entity to suit your personal circumstances.

With your business entity organised, your next step is to purchase or subscribe to an accounting package such as Xero or MYOB, and your accountant can assist you with this too. They can offer online support, training and assistance with the set-up of your business using your chosen software for easy processing of sales invoices, purchasing, stock, payroll, expenses and financial reporting. A good accountant will also help you answer the following key questions to make sure you understand the different options and implications of owning a business and to get you ready to start trading:

- What type of business structure should I use (sole trader/ company/trust/partnership)?

- What compliance do I need to have in place (GST registration/ BAS reporting/statutory reporting/PAYG tax)?

- What governance requirements need to be in place?

- Are there research and development (R&D) tax concessions available for my business and how do I track the R&D expenses to prepare a claim?

- How do I set up a payroll if I'm employing staff (payroll/ workers compensation/withholding tax/superannuation)?

- What insurances do I need (public liability/product liability/ professional indemnity/key person)?

In addition, you'll need to have a business dashboard in your accounting package so the key performance metrics for your business are in front of you when you log in. This will also provide you with quick online access to your financial statements (profit and loss, balance sheet and cash flow) for easy monitoring.

Executing the plan: Tobi's story

When the eBooks were launched, SWEAT quickly moved from several hundred clients to more than 1000 clients and then, after launching online, within 12 months they increased their reach to about 100 000 customers!

They discovered two critical things during this expansion:

- The existing feedback was being amplified due to the bigger numbers.

- As they internationalised, more specific and intricate problems arose around cultural and attitudinal discrepancies between one market and another.

Tobi talks about the difference in diversity between Australia and North America, for example, and states that 'lifestyles are different, and so the aspirations are different, and therefore the aesthetic goals can be different, and hence the attitudes and perspectives towards those aesthetic goals can be different'. There were also practical discrepancies, such as calories versus kilojoules and kilograms versus pounds, that had to be dealt with in the programs and updates to cater for all systems of measurement.

Tobi did note, however, that the fundamental pillars were consistent from one market to the other. It was intricate learning in bigger numbers that became a challenge, and with so many clients now using the system it was becoming impossible to read everything. This raised the question: 'How do you aggregate the insights?' Over time, they introduced more advanced processes and policies to extract those insights, and as time went on these were used to evolve the platform from the customer experience model (CX) through to customer support and a formal product management methodology, which created a philosophical shift in the business.

These were critical lessons in the execution and adjustment of Tobi's business plan to meet the market needs and adjust the operation to successfully manage rapid growth.

Executing the plan: Flavia's story

Flavia eventually found the application that was going to be the game changer for Fleet Space: mineral exploration. This sector was exploding in Australia, with rich deposits of critical minerals and rare earths that were in demand globally — nickel, lithium, copper, cobalt and graphite — all of which were needed for new technology batteries and solar panels. Flavia points out they are not interested in looking for further coal deposits or anything that is detrimental to carbon emissions or climate change, as fighting climate change is part of Fleet Space's company values.

The application that was perfect for Flavia's small satellite fleet was to undertake sub-surface scanning, looking for the right geographic formations, and to provide data quickly on areas that were prime for drilling. This is an application that creates an opportunity worth $10 billion a year for the mining sector!

As a result, in 2022 Fleet Space changed its focus completely to mining: 'It's not feasible for us to have non-mining customers. The process has been extremely painful and has taken years but eventually we got there', Flavia says.

Essentially...

- Validate your business model in the real world: are there customers who will pay, and what price?

- Understand how the business will operate and talk to potential suppliers and distribution channels if you're not going directly to the market.

- Create a forecast for the first three years of the business.

- Go over and over the numbers — sales, costs, margin, profit — with an accountant or mentor.

- Find an accountant who has experience with start-ups, and who you feel comfortable with, to assist you in getting the business fundamentals and compliance in place and to help you set up ready to trade from an accounting perspective.

CHAPTER 3

Product or service?

When deciding on the type of business you want to start (product or service), it's super important to understand in depth what you're getting yourself into, the ongoing effort required to run the business day to day and the perceived value of the business at the end of the day.

Will you have a physical product that can be mass produced and sold? Or will you provide a service, which could be anything from trash collection, hairdressing or pool cleaning through to a professional service such as accounting, marketing or industry consulting?

A service business is usually harder to take interstate or internationally as most of the costs and structure need to be replicated in each market you serve. In contrast, a product business, with the product being manufactured at one site, can sell easily to a global market if it has a unique differentiating advantage and can be available at any time in any time zone.

The main thing to consider is that if you're providing a service, you're only earning money when you or a staff member are physically working at $X per hour. This can be very draining both mentally and physically over time, and it's likely you'll end up 'becoming the business' and trading off your own good name, which can diminish the value of the business when you want to sell it or retire at some point in the future. The rule of thumb for a service business is that your salaried staff are charged out at three times their cost when working for clients, and billable hours become a constant performance metric, which is a constant stress in any service business.

It's because of this that service businesses are generally worth only one or two times their annual profit, whereas a product business can sell to its customers day and night, be mass produced and be replicated many times over. Additionally, it could sell for five to 10 times its annual profit, depending on future growth opportunities.

If you have a service business in mind, you may want to think about how you can 'productise' your service, possibly by creating a platform on which to expand your market and offering pre-formatted solutions day and night. These days, with digital platforms and marketing, the world is your market. You could write a book, or create a podcast series or online education tutorials that can be subscribed to (as Tobi and Kayla did: see the case study at the end of the chapter). The beauty of this is that you're creating a product from your service knowledge and an ongoing subscription income.

As you can see, there are incredible opportunities for service businesses. So take a minute to think about how you might best set up a service business so it has a complementary product platform or component that can take advantage of a broader market.

Businesses need to continually develop and grow to succeed long term, to keep pace with a rapidly changing world and to keep ahead of the competition, including new start-ups that will take your market if you let them.

Innovation and reinvention, as I talk about in this book, are key to long-term survival. You need to be continually thinking about how your product or service can be improved and refreshed, and your business efficiently expanded to serve new markets. Building this thinking into your initial business design will make for a much more flexible, healthy and valuable business long term.

SWEAT's successful productisation

The SWEAT story is a perfect example of productising a service. Productising their personal training enabled Tobi and Kayla to sell their PT programs to a global audience 24 hours a day. The important point here is that they were making enormous revenue while not actually working.

They took the business from personal training — which relied on Tobi working one-on-one with clients — to indoor group sessions with multiple clients training. Tobi repeatedly asked himself, 'How can I get more people to train at the same time?' and he was quite utilitarian in his approach: he moved the training sessions outdoors. When clients wanted to do more training at home, Tobi queried: 'How do I make money from that?' The answer was eBooks: low cost to produce and easy to sell direct to their client base. And before long, word of mouth had expanded their reach from around 100 to 1000 clients.

And that's not all. By being progressive, taking advantage of social media and seriously taking time to learn and understand the needs of their audience, SWEAT forged ahead and began producing video programs, which later evolved into the SWEAT app. The rest is history: within 12 months they had reached more than 100 000 consumers, with that number increasing to more than 50 million being reached with the SWEAT app by the time the business was sold to iFIT in 2021!

Essentially...

- Will your business be a product or a service?
- How can you 'productise' a service business to reach a broader customer base and create income when you're not physically working at it?

CHAPTER 4
Timing is everything

Having the right product or service (I'll call these the 'product' from here on in for simplicity) at the right time is essential when starting a business. You can have the best product in the world but if the world isn't ready for it, you'll face a high risk of failing.

If you need to educate the market you'll burn a lot of cash, and when starting a new business for the first time cash is usually a very limited commodity. If you run out, it's literally 'game over', both for the business and possibly for you personally as well, which can set you back a long way in life.

You might find that you're too late to the market because someone whose timing was perfect has beaten you to it. There's good and bad in that. On the bright side, they may have spent the money required to educate the market. However, they will have also taken the lead brand position, leaving you to play costly catch-up trying to position your brand over theirs. In addition, you'll have to do things better than them by further disrupting the market (see chapter 9 for everything you need to know about disruption).

Technology is a classic example. With technology you can do many incredible and wonderful things, but if the product or application you've developed doesn't solve a problem currently facing people or businesses, you're going nowhere fast. If you believe it does solve a problem, but people just don't know it yet, then you'll have to do a lot of educating, and getting the message through to the market will be expensive and must be carefully planned.

Our first family business, Regency Food Services, entered the market at a time when most takeaways, restaurants and hotels had many providers for every category of product. These included groceries, frozen foods, fresh meats, dairy, confectionery, salads, smallgoods and even packaging. We entered that market on the back of a trend we saw happening in the United States that we were also seeing signs of in the eastern states of Australia. The trend was called 'total foodservice'. It involved a rationalisation of the industry whereby the categories were combined under large, consolidated companies, providing the convenience of a 'one-stop' service to the customer. Regency Food Services was the first organisation to really bring the total foodservice concept together in South Australia and was well recognised nationally, winning Australian Foodservice Distributor of the Year in 1997. This positioned us extremely well when Bidvest, the first multinational in this sector, came into the market in the late 1990s and targeted our company for acquisition, resulting in a very successful sale in 1999.

My most recent venture, ZEN Energy, is another example of being in the right place at the right time. The company entered the market in 2004 when there were very few mainstream residential solar energy providers. At that time, articles on climate change were just starting to emerge in the newspapers and our prime minister, John Howard, was introducing the first subsidies for reducing carbon emissions in the home. The solar industry was still in the realms of 'weird science' for most people, who didn't understand the technology.

If you've done it yourself, you'll know that researching what's involved in installing a solar energy system in your home—wondering what components to choose, who should install it and how to claim a rebate—can be confusing and time consuming. What the industry lacked at the time was a fully branded and integrated home solar energy system where the company and the components used were completely trusted. It was an opportunity to pioneer a new industry and create the leading brand in the market.

Initially, we called the company ZEN Home Energy Systems. We brought together manufacturers to produce the components under our brand and to match the high-quality components into a fully integrated system for the residential market. We kept the offering simple, going to market with four systems that powered from one-quarter to all of the average home. It was a brand that people loved and could identify with, but most importantly it took away the need to understand the technology and instead delivered it to the market with a simple choice of systems that people trusted.

Having the right product in the market at the right time resulted in the company reaching dizzying levels of growth over the first few years. While the rest of the world was going through the global financial crisis, ZEN was achieving year-on-year growth in excess of 400 per cent, winning Australian Entrepreneur of the Year in 2010 for the Cleantech sector and reaching number 4 on *BRW*'s list of fastest growing companies in Australia.

The lesson here is that timing is critical and having the right product at the right time raises your chances of success enormously.

If you're not sure of the market timing, you need to revisit your validation model and conduct further research with your potential customers to understand whether they would buy your product, and whether they would buy it at the price you believe you could deliver it for. This might mean going back to the drawing board a number of times to get the product fit and market acceptance to a demand level that makes it viable to launch your product. You must also consider barriers to entry so that people can't easily copy what you're doing, whether this is for protection of your intellectual property or your business model in the form of a patent. This also applies to protecting your brand and logo by applying for a trademark (I'll elaborate on this in chapter 13).

Timing really was everything for SWEAT

The convergence of technology, lifestyle and fitness provided the perfect timing for a business like SWEAT to evolve. As Tobi says, 'Everything happens in cycles'.

The fitness industry can be broken down into:

- retail (gyms and personal training)
- hardware (equipment)
- product content
- combinations of the above.

Tobi recalls:

> Our timing was fortunate as there were a couple of big trends happening at the same time. Retail had gone from 'Big Box' expensive gyms to 24/7 moderate-service but convenience-focused gyms as the whole industry realised convenience was key. There was also the realisation that preference, variability and variety were becoming more interesting, which saw the rise of 'pop-up' style fitness boutiques, which also became popular.

> This meant 'specificity' was of high value and SWEAT was hyper-specific: we were female only, largely high intensity, very targeted outcome and we knew who we were targeting.

They also knew that the internet, and more broadly 'digital', was becoming a thing, and they didn't have to use 'crappy infomercials to sell dodgy DVDs' that presented the 'get abs in 30 days type of junk'. Tobi laughs and says, 'I train a lot but I doubt that I could get abs in 30 days!'

They were able to develop the product/service mechanism with the new tech enablement and digitisation that was happening combined with the ability to get to market on social media, which many competitors didn't yet understand — yet their business really grew up with it.

There was also a massive attitudinal shift bubbling away in the background, with women in particular getting very tired of the aesthetic stigma that existed in the media — that training was all about having a 'thigh gap' or 'being slim' or 'this or that' — when what women really wanted was just to feel good and feel confident.

If you look at the intersection of all those things, there was an aggregation of opportunity in both the demand and supply aspects of the business. In Tobi's words:

> We were able to build digitised supply at very low cost to get started with low barriers to entry. We were able to supply product and content in a way that hadn't been done before so we were ahead of the market. From a demand perspective we had accessed some new channels where our audience was that were still really in their infancy as far as the business models were concerned. Facebook advertising had really only just begun, videos weren't even on Instagram, messaging wasn't on Instagram — it didn't exist!

Tobi continues,

> We could see it evolving and we persisted, knowing it was right for our business model. It's often difficult for founders to extract themselves out of the position they are in to see the bigger or biggest picture.

The timing was perfect for Fleet Space

Flavia admits that:

> ... the timing was good for us. If you look at Silicon Valley, every single billionaire in software was investing in space, and with more computing power and much smaller and lighter hardware, suddenly you can launch satellites into space at a much lower cost.

> Silicon Valley has woken up quickly to this new thing called 'Space' and [are] making billions of dollars on space technology because of a couple of people who have now created the opportunity.

Flavia also makes the comment that adding to this timing is climate change, which is leaving a trail of disaster for all enterprises across the planet, and space technology is now coming to the rescue.

A mix of bad and good timing
for Haigh's expansion

The first big growth Haigh's had was when they opened in Sydney in 2005 (their second attempt) and into the Strand Arcade. Jurlique was moving stores as it needed more space for treatment rooms and the corner site became an opportunity that Haigh's took up before it even went to market. The rent was high, and John Haigh thought his sons Simon and Alister were mad for paying so much. But that store became their highest turnover store nationally within 18 months!

Simon says, 'We were totally underprepared for it'. Haigh's had strong brand recognition in Adelaide and Melbourne, and they had failed to predict the number of ex-Adelaide and ex-Melbourne people who had moved to Sydney and the resulting brand recognition that quickly came with that. Haigh's just wasn't geared up to produce the amount of stock that the new Sydney store was adding, and for six to eight months they were playing catch-up just to service the demand as queues at the Strand store were out the door. Capacity wise, this drove everything else within the business to grow and keep up.

Their original launch into the Sydney market was tied in with the failed launch of the Georges of Melbourne department store into Sydney. Georges was a Melbourne institution and a true Emporium, providing exclusive goods and meticulous service, before it was sold to the David Jones department store business in 1981. David Jones later tried to replicate the culture of Georges and launch the brand in Sydney, but sadly the uniqueness of the brand was lost on the Sydney market, and just didn't work under the David Jones national operational model. Haigh's, which was a key feature of the Melbourne format of the store, initially went into Sydney as part of the Georges launch and was subsequently caught up in the failure of the two Georges sites, one at Double Bay and the other on the 7th floor of the David Jones store in Elizabeth Street.

You can't always choose your timing, but it's something you need to be prepared for. As a company, Haigh's has always stayed nimble and responded to opportunities as they emerge, learning key lessons in being prepared along the way. Simon says, 'It may not always be the best decision, but we must be able to make quick decisions when an opportunity arises'. Sydney (second time around) became the new focus, with plenty of demand — in fact, the second Sydney store, which opened two years later, was positioned only 500 metres away in the Queen Victoria Building. Haigh's now has seven stores in Sydney, one in Canberra, seven in Melbourne and seven in Adelaide.

The Canberra store was an example of being prepared. The shopping centre was a new type of centre that had a clearly defined gift area and associated experience, which is what Haigh's shops are best suited to. The centre operators approached Haigh's, and the location was seen as a perfect match for the brand. The store was designed, approved and built within two months — a record for Haigh's!

Essentially...

- Is the market ready for your business?

- If you're too early, it will cost a large amount to educate the consumer.

- If you're too late, it will cost a large amount to catch up to your competitors.

- If you're not sure whether the market timing is right, revisit your validation model and conduct further research.

CHAPTER 5

Passion, culture and values

To create, re-invent or disrupt an industry takes an inordinate amount of energy. If you're creating a business purely for financial reasons it will become a job; and take it from me: the energy you have for the job and to drive change will diminish over time.

People who create and change industries are passionate people, and you'll need every inch of that passion to manoeuvre the obstacles that will be thrown up to stop you from achieving your goals.

The more complex the industry, the more obstacles you'll come across, and the more energy and drive you'll need, so be very careful when choosing your business or industry and objectives to ensure you have the internal fortitude to carry it through.

If you're fortunate enough to achieve early success and your business model is working roughly as planned, then be ready for the copycats to be right on your heels. When people see a good idea work, they will quickly rally the troops to have a crack at the same market and often even try and leverage off not just your business model but also your branding—so make sure your business model and brand are both protected by patents and trademarks.

ZEN Home Energy Systems was very successful very early, and suddenly out of the blue all of these other ZEN businesses started emerging. Fortunately, we had trademarked not only our logo, but also the word 'ZEN' for the three trademark categories relevant to our business. For a while we seemed to be sending out 'cease and desist' letters every week to people trying to leverage off our brand. As soon as we stopped one, another would start up! And then there were the people just trying to copy our business.

Being first to market is an important position to hold and it requires continual innovation and improvement in your business model to hold at bay the wolves who will be biting at your heels. This will be exhausting—you'll want to have enormous passion and energy for what you've created to stay in front.

My passion for pioneering the renewable energy sector in Australia and the generation and storage of clean energy, together with the changes required in the electricity markets to enable this new technology and create a better future for our children, was the drive that kept me going through all the challenges in this business.

To be successful, you'll need to recruit people who share your values and want to go on that same journey with you: to innovate and move the world forward, which is the fundamental basis for creating a culture to succeed within your business.

The business architecture stack

It's important to give your business a 'personality': to define who you are, your mission, your brand, your values and your tagline(s). This profile is sometimes referred to as a 'business architecture stack': it's the 'why' you get out of bed every morning, and the 'why' you exist, and can be used in business documents and job descriptions to attract and motivate employees, to build consistency within your business and brand, and to share your corporate values with the outside world.

Figure 5.1 presents an early version of ZEN Energy's architecture stack. You can clearly see the aspirational nat mission statement. It didn't say what we sell or how we do it, ~~it created~~ the 'why' we exist, which is then translated into our vision and core values, leading to the culture and personality of our business.

Mission	Show our customers how to 'Live Free' in a Zero ENergy environment				
Vision	To build Australia's leading renewable energy brand				
Core values	Innovation and thirst for learning	Market leadership	Customer care and service	Trust and respect	Honesty and integrity
Positioning statement	ZEN is 'Zero ENergy' (balancing energy generation and storage with consumption) and carries the Eastern connotations of 'enlightenment, wisdom and a new way of life'				
Value proposition	To provide Australia's first **fully branded** and **integrated** renewable energy generation and storage systems produced by the world's leading component manufacturers and supported by the highest standards of **customer service** and **installation.**				
Taglines	'Live Free with ZEN' and 'Blue is the new Green'				

Figure 5.1: an early version of ZEN Energy's business architecture stack

Use this as a guide to shape your own thinking. It's not necessary to have it all written down from day one because your passion and excitement will exude out of you when you talk with people and this will attract your core group of initial employees naturally—like bees to a honeypot. But you must still have an awareness of the company culture you want to create. At some point early on, together with your team, you need to commit these principles to writing and have everyone on board, committed and focused on achieving the company's mission. You can also use this as the basis for regular reviews of your business plan with your team and review your 'why' and the mission, vision and values together with the team, getting everyone's input and ensuring your people are still deeply committed to the purpose.

Keeping the passion alive

As your business grows with more employees, particularly if you're working in different locations and rely on other people for recruitment, it becomes much harder to personally share your passion. It's almost impossible for other people to purvey the same passion and excitement that you do, which is why you have to write it down.

Sometimes leaders of larger organisations will do it via personal videos sent to staff regularly celebrating successes that may name people personally who have contributed to the organisation and have demonstrated the company values.

Creating a great culture isn't always easy, and more often than not it takes a lot of time and demonstrated effort for your team to believe that it's real. As hard as it can be to build a great culture, it can be torn down very easily and quickly by disgruntled, toxic people who have become disenchanted with the business or management one way or another. When this happens, you must act quickly to talk to the person or persons involved and contain the issue. If this can't be done, consider other options including a personal development plan, or failing that, the process to manage them appropriately out of the business.

Failing to take action with people who demonstrate poor company values, even though they might be high performers, is actually disrespecting your other staff and you will soon lose key team members. It amazes me to see the relief in a team when a toxic person is removed, and it further amazes me to see the people who quickly step up to take on responsibility when that person is gone.

Remember, if you walk past poor behaviour that's outside of the company values and do nothing, you're accepting that behaviour and condoning it in front of your staff, which is a quick way to destroy the culture and the hard work you're doing in other parts of the business to build the culture and the aspirations that you and the team want to achieve.

SWEATing the passion, culture and values

Tobi says: 'How many times have you heard about a great 300-page planning document that sits in the draw and no-one ever looks at?'

Vision, purpose and values sit at the heart of SWEAT. There was a part of SWEAT in every single position description and job advertisement that went out. When people were recruited, the vision, purpose and values would be in the Q&A list as part of the interview. If you got the job, and as part of the onboarding process, which carried the fitness theme of 'start strong', Tobi would personally present to you. This session with Tobi was run monthly or quarterly, depending on how many new employees had come on over a period of time. He would present his overall perspective on the vision, purpose and values, and then the other managers would come in and similarly present their perspectives on the culture in relation to their part of the business.

Tobi used the OKR (objectives and key results) methodology for performance assessment. Both 'culture' and 'development' were categorised as OKRs that people had to have, and their performance would be managed against these. They would have monthly 'town halls' called 'SWEAT Connect' with the vision, purpose and values communicated at the beginning of every presentation. The aim of these presentations was to connect the team to where they were going. There would be a strategic session with a business headline and industry headline from Tobi as the CEO, a performance update from the CFO, an operational update from the COO, a 'People and Culture' (PandC) update featuring awards for staff tenure, most voted for person of the month and a summary of client results from their community. They would reach out to customers who had great stories, which were recorded and played at the presentations so that the whole company could see the impact

(continued)

they were making on people's lives. The SWEAT Connect sessions were also recorded and sent to staff who couldn't attend, along with Uber Eats vouchers so they could eat while they watched!

Tobi admits that their ability to report on the things discussed during the SWEAT Connect sessions in the early days was terrible and they learned as they went, developing as fast as they could. The goal was to leave 'no stone unturned' in achieving the culture they wanted, and as their systems became more sophisticated later in the company's development, they wanted everyone to be connected and to know the strategy and the company's performance, to be in sync with the business, to be engaged and to be performing at their best.

The interpretation of engagement and motivation was different for everyone: some were engaged by money, some were engaged by a better desk, some were engaged by flexibility. The company became more 'flexible' with working hours over time and with experience. Tobi admits he was probably the biggest blocker to flexibility early on. In 2015 Tobi was the leader of the 9 to 5 Monday to Friday crusade. They then introduced flexible start and finish times and then ultimately moved to become fully flexible with a few 'fixed hours a day' put aside as a window for meetings that you had to be available for. Other than that, the hours became very flexible. They had staff, for example, who would visit distant family for six weeks and work from the family's home subject to this being signed off and approved.

Tobi learned over time while trying to set up everything to be structured and process driven to 'get things right', that in a subliminal way he was implying that the company didn't trust them. As a result, they took themselves through the thought process that if they did trust them and no-one ever did the wrong thing, what would that look like? The outcome of that process was that 'well and truly' the minority of people do silly things. Sometimes there's an expectation gap, but that normally self-corrects over time.

The trade-off that you get from letting go with the trust that you get allows you to apply a higher degree of accountability. As you will see shortly, Tobi now agrees with Flavia on the alignment of values and flexibility, adding that it's much easier to start with that and then improve on it than it is to start with nothing and try to build something that then becomes a much bigger cultural shift, which SWEAT had to go through over four to five years. They even had a 'Culture Committee', which had a budget and an aspirational objective to move the team even closer to SWEAT's values. The aim was to make it ever present, everywhere. Even with people being based overseas Tobi talks about the 'operating rhythm' being the 'heartbeat of the business' so that structure and rhythm are maintained in all offices.

Tobi says:

> At a high level and now as the business is maturing, all teams are working directionally towards an annual plan, then quarterly meetings to review that and adjust as necessary, then monthly reviewing of your own performance against that, then either weekly or fortnightly there are individual meetings or WIPS that keep the heartbeat going.

Passion, culture and values are not fleeting for Flavia

> We are passionate leaders with a clear vision, and we infuse this into our staff every day, so everyone knows it. You see it everywhere as you walk around Fleet. Our vision is to put a constellation of satellites around the Earth, Moon and Mars.

To Flavia, it's not a small goal, it's a *big* goal. And Fleet doesn't stop repeating it over and over again. Flavia states:

> If you come here, you are an 'explorer' and you want to move with us on this mission. This about saving the Earth, Moon and Mars: 'exploring', not 'exploiting'. We have a stand that we are not going to work with oil companies or coal companies; we are simply not going to work with exploiters.

(continued)

45

We are going to build the best technologies; our mining technology is purposefully passive to avoid unnecessary drilling creating an ethical way of exploring for critical mineral deposits. Exploration is part of being human, but exploitation is also a part: the part that unnecessarily destroys the ecosystem. We talk about this all the time and how we can use our technologies to avoid exploitation, both on Earth and also as we build our plans to visit other planets.

People would historically work to stay alive, buy food and provide shelter for their families. Our parents and grandparents, though, were among the first generations working for wealth, working to buy a house, to buy a car and go on holidays. This current younger generation don't see that as their primary purpose, they have food and parents who have done well. They want 'freedom and purpose' and that's it, aligning with their personal values. Mental health is also of critical importance so flexibility in the workplace is of the utmost importance.

Flavia is very passionate when she says:

You can work anywhere, you can do whatever you want at any time of the day as long as you achieve this, and I'm going to take care of you and talk to you, pay for your health care, pay for your husband to look after your child. People want to lead a good, purposeful life. That's how I see this point in time ...

Keeping the passion and culture over generations at Haigh's

The Haigh's staff have a very deep connection with the history and tradition of chocolate making at Haigh's and the Haigh's brand. Simon also credits having a great executive team for a long period who have been heavily involved in the strategic planning for the business and working this through with the staff.

Simon believes 'being a family business helps this evolution, as they have always looked after the people who have been part of the Haigh's journey'. Many staff have been in for the long haul, with 25 staff or more in the 20-year service club, and one staff member even at 40 years of service. Simon admits it's been an interesting ride across generations. When Alister and Simon came in as the fourth generation, and being kids growing up in the business, it was a challenge for long-term staff who were used to working under John Haigh. Accepting the new, young management wasn't easy for everyone and some hard decisions were made as the years went on.

With both Alister and Simon starting to approach semi-retirement and working less in the business, and the business never having a formal board until now (only family members), work is now underway to commence the process of setting up a formal board for the first time to bridge the strategic management across to a potential fifth generation family member as they emerge.

Essentially...

- You must have a passion for the business you are in to continue to innovate and lead an industry.

- From your passion, mission and vision you must create a culture and value set for your organisation and look for people who align with that culture and share the vision.

- Constantly reward team members who demonstrate your company culture.

- Take action quickly if a team member becomes toxic and demonstrates poor values and culture.

CHAPTER 6

Brand positioning and marketing

In this chapter you'll learn about the importance of positioning your brand in the market so the right customers can find you, undertaking market research to understand who your customer is and how to reach them, and then how to motivate them to make that all-important enquiry.

Just a reminder that I use the term 'product' when I talk about a product or service, just to keep things simple.

The brand

A good brand must say what you do, or at least have a tagline that does. Clever dual meanings that encompass your values work well, but be careful with made-up and misspelt words as people need to be able to find you, and educating the market about some made-up name costs a lot of money. If people can't find you or don't know you exist when searching for a product it can be a fast track to business failure.

Brand positioning in a crowded market space is a critical part of the process. Do you picture your brand as an aspirational or luxury brand at a premium price, and if so how will this be justified (through luxury design, or features or both)? How will this impact the sales model: will it be at a high price point with a high margin due to the quality, design and complexity of the product and possibly as a result limited to a niche wealthier market and a lower sales volume? A luxury brand has to look, feel and function like a luxury product and there are plenty of examples out there across the fashion, automobile and other sectors to model your brand on. Will your brand be an affordable (mid-market) brand with appeal to the everyday person in the street, or will it be a necessary everyday item? Will it be an irregular purchase or will it be a budget item aiming for sales volume at a low price point and low margin? This all needs to be carefully considered when determining your position in the market, who your customers are and how to engage with them — what's more, this also impacts heavily on your business planning in terms of the sales and revenue model.

In marketing we talk about getting a test group of potential customers together to test all aspects of your product, particularly the messaging you'll use in your communications, which should aim to trigger an emotive response and engage them. Your brand is at the forefront of this message and will usually be the first thing they see in an advertisement, in a store or online so it needs to be impactful, meaningful, relatable and memorable.

My first company was Regency Food Services. The name 'Regency' has many global associations to high-end hospitality venues and hospitality training, and the fact we were located in Regency Park and near the Regency Hospitality Training College carried that nice dual meaning, which made it memorable to our customers and worked exceptionally well for that business. When the business extended into hospitality labour hire, we used the name Regency Staffing, which performed equally well for us.

ZEN Home Energy Systems, and its transition to ZEN Energy, was exceptional as it encapsulated everything we wanted in a renewable energy brand. It was an acronym for Zero Energy (balancing generation and demand) and it carried those beautiful Eastern connotations of wisdom, enlightenment and a new way of life. People instantly connected with the brand and our mission towards energy independence and the brand quickly became top of mind in the renewable energy sector.

So do what you need to do to get yourself into that creative thinking mode: a good bottle of red with some friends or a long hot shower to get the brain working usually does it for me! And get thinking about a creative, imaginative and unique brand that will be memorable for your business. There's a balance between unique and functional: you want the brand to be as unique as possible, so it ranks high in the search results but without losing the essence of what you are. This can be overcome to a degree with searchable keywords on websites, for instance, but searchable words in the title generally yield the best results. If you were searching for home energy at that time, you would have usually found ZEN Home Energy Systems at the top of the list.

Get a test group of potential customers together and test some brand ideas out on them, listen carefully and note the feedback. In most sessions I've been involved with there's usually one brand that jumps out and provides the 'ah ha' moment... but if not, it's back to the drawing board to continue working on the ideas, taking on the feedback. The brand will be with you for a long time, hopefully, so you need it to be strong—remember: *impactful, meaningful, relatable and memorable!*

Once you settle on a brand and have checked that it doesn't clash with any other business names (check the ASIC website in Australia) and that you can secure the web domain and other relevant social media pages, the next job is to design the logo and tagline and then protect the combined elements.

First impressions are so important and a professional-looking brand is critical for credibility. I have always done a lot of work upfront in my brand designs and engaged a graphic designer to produce a logo, tagline and associated 'style guide', which details how the brand is to be represented in all media platforms for consistency. If the colours are wrong, or the logo is stretched thin or wide and it looks like you couldn't afford a graphic designer, people won't trust your business. Always look professional and consistent when presenting to the market.

Investing in your logo design upfront also avoids the need to improve it constantly as your business grows. Once you start trading, you're invested in your logo, so you may want to protect it and potentially trademark it to prevent other businesses leveraging off your brand and success (see chapter 13 for more on this), but if you continually change it as your business develops you may also void your trademark and lose the protection.

Marketing

There are two very different and important sides to marketing. One is the research side, where you're learning about who your customer is and how to connect with them, and the other is the creative side, which is the resulting design of the marketing material to engage the customer based on what you've learned from the research.

Do you reach out to them directly through advertising (either traditionally through TV, press and radio, or on digital and social media platforms) or do you do it more discreetly via public relations or influencers (other people talking about and endorsing your product on their own platforms). Marketing is the tool used to generate initial interest in a product and to spark the customer into researching the offering. Usually, the marketing would direct them to a website, brochures or a retail store where they can learn more and start engaging with the sales channel.

Researching your market

The research side of marketing is understanding who your customer is and how to communicate with them. What is their gender and age?

Where are they located? What are their interests? What media do they consume? What will motivate them to buy your product? You need to determine how you're going to reach them with information about your new product in a way that's going to engage them and inspire them to make an inquiry. Importantly, your research should look closely at what your competitors are doing: what their approach is to the market and their 'value proposition' for the customer. What channels are they using to reach their customer. How much marketing are they doing and how much are they spending? You need to clearly understand *your* competitive strengths versus your competitors' and ensure that point of difference is projected strongly in your marketing material. Understanding in detail where you can bring value to the customer and your competitors can't, and encapsulating that within your marketing material, is essential for success.

Large corporations spend an enormous amount of money on market research, which plays a major role in the overall field of marketing. They will generally engage market research firms to analyse huge amounts of media data and sales data as well as conduct focus groups to assist corporations to understand everything they know — *and* don't know — about their potential customers, but through very complex statistical analysis of real-life available data.

This information then feeds into their marketing program development from mainstream advertising campaigns in traditional TV, radio and press through to digital advertising and communications via social media platforms and their influencers. They will use the data to identify what keywords to use in websites for search engine optimisation (SEO) and what Adwords (that is, key words you should use in Google ads) to use with search engines to ensure their websites are found when those keywords are typed in. They will know exactly who they are targeting, where and how to reach them, and what inspires their potential customers to take action and enquire to find out more. They will also, as I mentioned earlier, gain a lot of information about their competitors, where they are advertising, who they are advertising to, what their messaging is and how much they are spending.

Testing out your customer

In start-up land I don't expect you to spend millions of dollars on complex market research to understand who your customer is, but you *do* need to know that you have a customer and validate that they are willing to pay the price for your product. What would trigger an emotive response that would inspire them to make an enquiry?

A good place to start this process is with family and friends. You will certainly have an idea in your mind as to who your customer is, so this process is about validating your thinking, testing the product and the price point, and above all, getting feedback that you can use to fine tune your product and marketing plan. Then keep testing until your audience is satisfied and guarantees they would buy the product at the price you believe it can be delivered. Next, take pre-orders (never waste an opportunity for sales!).

Testing could involve a group of about ten family and friends. Here's how to go about it:

- Ask the right (open-ended) questions to get a detailed response.

- Understand the problems in their lives that the product is solving.

- Find out if the product could help them in other ways that you haven't thought of: is the product going to benefit them the way you really think it is?

- Talk about colours, size, shape, design and functionality. There may be other features or applications you haven't considered.

- Ask them who, in their opinion, are the potential competitors in the market.

Now these are family and friends, so the next step might be to broaden the test group (known as a focus group in marketing) and get them to suggest other people they know who would be interested, to ensure they are not just being nice to you. People you don't know will be more likely give you honest answers and more detailed feedback. Do the improvement cycle and then call another session — and keep refining. It can be very frustrating work and often it's not what you want to hear, but that's better than losing a lot of money in a failed business attempt.

As well as testing your product concept and price point, and understanding your customers at a deeper level, it's essential to ensure the values of your brand (aligned with your mission and company culture) connect at an emotive level with your customers. After all, it's the emotive level of the brain that will trigger the buying response and the connection to your brand. Your customers need to relate and connect to your journey, your passion and 'why' you get out of bed in the morning—that is, the values that your business must be built on, as we discussed in the previous chapter.

It's this fundamental understanding of your customer that will form the building blocks of developing the way you communicate with them. There's a brilliant TED Talk video by marketing guru Simon Sinek that you can look up on 'Why' you do what you do, compared to 'What' you do and 'How' you do it, which clearly demonstrates the emotive triggers of why people connect to your brand and not others. I've put a link to the video on the companion website to the book for easy reference (www.essentialentrepreneur.com).

Once you build a deeper relationship with your test market and begin to understand who your customer is, it's time to ascertain what media they consume, and when, in order for the marketing you develop to reach them at the right time, in the right place, maximising the impact of your spend. Traditional media in TV, radio or the press can be expensive so you don't want to use a trial-and-error process to see what works. Digital media, including social media and influencers, is generally more cost effective, but again you must have that cut-through emotional connection as it's a very congested space, and you must know what platforms to use and when to reach your customer to minimise your spend and maximise your impact.

Designing a campaign

The next step is to design a campaign to attract your first customers. As I've already mentioned, I always engage a commercial graphic designer with a marketing background to design the content for my marketing campaign so that it looks professional and consistent with my branding and positioning in the market. People don't know if you're a start-up or an early stage business and you want to gain trust immediately, so credibility and looking professional is essential (this must apply to everything to do with your business). The number of companies around with poor-quality, amateur-looking marketing material and presentations continually astounds me—they're setting themselves up for failure. You've come this far so let's get the execution right.

If you want sales, you'll need a 'call to action' to ensure you get a response that drives potential customers to your website, or to pick up the phone and call. Then you need to convert that inquiry into a sale. You may have to set the scene in your marketing to educate your customer in the value of your product to create that all-important emotive response, so draw on the lessons you learned from your focus group testing to ensure each piece of your campaign is producing the right response.

Once you've designed your marketing material and you know where your customers are, what media they are consuming and when, you can purchase advertising space directly from the media source in most cases. The other alternative is to talk to an advertising agency, which is also an option for building your campaign if you have more money to spend. Advertising agencies have media buyers and data to show exactly where your customers are, and part of their business is buying blocks of targeted advertising space at significantly cheaper prices—however, this is usually for a sizeable campaign and spend. What's more, they can tell you what your competitors are doing and what they're spending—which is handy if you want a comparison.

The marketing cycle

Marketing your product involves a full cycle, beginning with market research, product development, marketing, sales, product feedback, product improvements or updates (product cycles) and even product range extensions right through to re-launching and marketing new features. A product's life can be relatively short if it's following a short-term trend (remember those fidget spinners a few years back?) so you want to maximise your immediate impact and sales. Alternatively, it could have a much longer life with a slower build, meaning the entire cycle, including enhancements, becomes much longer. Product improvements or updates must be tested as well and should be based on feedback from your customers (again not just what you think) so that you know it will appeal to your broader market and attract more customers.

Engaging some PR help

Another form of marketing that I find particularly useful when building a public profile for my businesses and taking consumers on my personal journey is public relations (PR). This entails engaging journalists directly from the media or blogs to write or produce stories on you, your company or both. Or you might be called on for comment as the industry expert for a topical story on whatever industry sector you're in.

It's hard to do this directly as it's unlikely you have personal relationships with many journalists. That's where PR companies come in. Working with a PR company can be a cost-effective way to have credible stories written about you and your success, which is a better option than doing your own marketing where you talk about yourself and your products.

PR companies work closely with journalists right across the media spectrum. They will write topical stories about you and/or your company and products and feed these to targeted journalists at the appropriate time so they have the best chance of being published. They will also continually be in contact with journalists and listen out for stories that you or your company could be featured in or that you could comment on. Usually, when anything came up in the news about renewable energy or home energy, I'd be called up by the PR company and they would organise for the journalist to call me directly for comment.

If something ever goes wrong with your business, PR companies can also be engaged for 'damage control'. They can manage the media and attempt to limit the damage to your business, yourself and your family by communicating on your behalf or prompting you with the right words to say at a media conference to diffuse a situation.

People occasionally tell me they like to fly under the radar, but if you continually operate under the radar you'll probably fall off the radar scope one day. It's always important to talk about your successes, but most importantly it's better to have someone else with credibility talk about your successes publicly.

* * *

Marketing can be a lot of fun and really engages the creative side of your thinking and personality, but where possible draw on some expert support in both the research and design sides and remember to present your business professionally. That first impact and impression is the key to success.

The evolution of SWEAT as a brand

Tobi's no-nonsense approach served SWEAT's needs when they were evolving their brand. What would a brand look like? Tobi declares that

Tech companies are a thing. I like fitness, but I love business. We were adding a tremendous amount of positive impact to the world in our category, but what more could we do? And what more could the business do if it had more resources?

Digital technology went from desktop to mobile; content quality went from low and crappy to medium and heading towards high quality; streaming was freeing itself from buffering and heading from low to medium and, more recently, high quality.

The brand started as 'SWEAT with Kayla', which carried significant key person risk and was always going to limit the growth of the business and its ability to be saleable at some point. As things progressed, Tobi learned to be very focused on the end game and setting the business up to exit. He says that it is so important from the very early stages of any business start-up to be focused on the exit and how that can happen.

To enable this, the next iteration of the brand introduced other fitness instructors and the brand moved from 'SWEAT with Kayla' to 'SWEAT with whoever the instructor was', and then eventually the 'with' was dropped and the brand evolved into simply 'SWEAT'.

The importance of brand and design to Fleet Space

Flavia feels their brand is strong and slick and she's a huge believer in the importance of great graphic design for any business, but for Fleet Space, which was trailblazing a new space industry, it had to be perfect. She says Matt (Fleet's co-founder) has 'massive vision' and incredible style. After six months, Matt took control of every presentation and every brochure: 'no one touches this' he said. Up until recently, he had been doing everything himself, not trusting anyone else to take on the marketing side of the business until he 'finally hired a marketing team that he didn't let go after 2 minutes', says Flavia. Matt's quality of styling, elegance, class and consistency is so high and of such excellent quality that Flavia believes he is a key reason why Fleet is thriving.

Fleet is all about telling stories, and Matt's creative work is imperative for their success. Now it's getting even slicker and sharper ...

Haigh's market research on products and store locations

Haigh's is constantly working on new products and actively seeking customer feedback. Often, the greatest amount of feedback comes when they discontinue a line because it's always someone's favourite... and sometimes that someone is an upset radio personality!

Haigh's undertakes market research on new products coming onto the market, both locally and internationally. The product development team creates many variations of potential new products. These are taste-tested by the factory team and staff for comments and suggestions for improvement.

Simon says, 'There is not a lot of scope for product innovation with chocolate. Even the bigger companies don't manage to innovate much'. Instead, they will try to extend the life cycle of their successful brands and products for as long as possible by adding further product variations to an already proven and successful brand or range. Not many have come up with a totally new product in recent years. Kit Kat is an example of a historically successful product that now has about twenty variations and it's the same with many other products. There are no significant new products coming onto the market apart from some of the new 'ruby chocolates' that have appeared in recent years. In fact, some old brands that had disappeared from the market years ago are making a nostalgic comeback, and old production lines are being repurchased and restarted, which is an interesting market development, much like the cyclic nature of fashion and music.

New stores and locations are extensively researched for the right demographics within a geographic area and within shopping centres. Software is now available to study the traffic flows and revenues to determine the right shop location with the potential to produce the required revenues.

Simon talks about the evolution of shopping centres and says, 'Historically, shopping centres have been difficult to work with and not interested in building relationships. Their loyalty usually went to the highest bidder, not necessarily the longest and most loyal tenants'. Haigh's found that out the hard way when, in one popular location, their lease was terminated after 20 years in favour of a growing national chain that wanted the site. Shopping centres would use the 'churn factor' knowing that if you go bust there will always be someone else to take your place. They would also insist on a refit every five years so everything you made in that period went into the refit.

As a result, Haigh's moved into 'strip shopping', where they had a stronger long-term relationship with the landlords, and opened many successful standalone stores in both Adelaide and Melbourne, avoiding shopping centres for a lengthy period. In recent years, however, Haigh's started moving into them again, as the competition for shopping centres is now firmly against online shopping, and as a result they are finding new value in working with the best retailers, which provide unique 'in-store' experiences. Simon says, 'Shopping centres have changed their attitude. They now value solid tenants and are most accommodating when working with good tenants to achieve the best possible outcomes for all parties'.

Another interesting observation was around what suburbs had enough disposable income to support a profitable store. Some up-and-coming suburbs during the 1980s had highly mortgaged, large houses, with people struggling to furnish the house, let alone afford the luxury of premium chocolate — or often anything else for that matter. Haigh's demographic research then looked at regions where disposable income was higher and could support their retail stores.

Essentially ...

- A good brand must say what you do, or at least have a tagline that does.

- Clever dual meanings that encompass your values work well, but be careful with made-up and misspelt words as people need to be able to find you.

- Where does your brand sit in the market? Is it defined as 'luxury', 'affordable', 'essential'? Is it high price and low volume or low price and high volume, or does it sit in the middle of the market?

- Test the brand on your potential customers and keep fine tuning until it triggers the right values alignment and emotional response.

- There are two sides to marketing: market research, which seeks to understand who your customers are, where are they and how you will best communicate with them; and the creative side, where you create the content and messaging to trigger the emotive buying response you are seeking in order to prompt your potential customer to engage with your sales channels.

- A worthwhile alternative to standard advertising (where you are directly communicating with your potential customers) is to use a PR company to engage credible third parties to talk and write about your company through more traditional channels along with social media influencers.

- Ensure there is a feedback loop to survey customers on their engagement with your business, as well as their product experience, so you can use your market research to continually improve the customer experience and service.

CHAPTER 7

Bringing in those sales

In chapter 6 we touched on the importance of creating an effective and well-targeted marketing campaign that triggers the desired emotive enquiry. Next we'll discover the importance of how your business engages with the customer when they make that enquiry to convert it into an all-important sale.

Converting marketing enquiries into sales

Once you capture leads and enquiries through your marketing, the next critical phase, which lets many businesses down, is converting that lead or enquiry into a sale. This is where the 'tread meets the road', as they say, and where the enthused potential customer actually gets to engage and experience their first impressions of dealing with your business. First impressions are like a first date: you may have a great photo and profile on the dating app, but if you lose them when you open your mouth it's not going to be a good night!

That first engagement with your website, retail store or salesperson needs to reinforce the brand values and the brand positioning that you have portrayed in your marketing. This is what got them there in the first place so make sure you keep it consistent throughout the entire experience.

If it's a website that they're directed to, it must look professional and the layout must be clear and functional. Your potential customers need to be able to quickly find the information they want to learn more about, and it must be presented in a clear and engaging way, again re-enforcing your brand values (the 'Why' you exist) so they align with your customer's personal values and hopefully trigger that emotive purchase. If it's a retail store, the experience, look and layout must reflect the same brand positioning, values and functionality. The same goes for mobile sales people, and so on.

Pricing techniques

There are many techniques where pricing is used in conjunction with the product and its benefits to attract and convert a sale. This may have been used in your marketing to get a potential customer to your website or physical store, or you may have kept the price from public view until an enquiry was made, or you might have asked the customer to enter some personal data first to build your database.

You would have experienced many different pricing strategies in your day-to-day shopping life. For example, there are low-cost 'get you into the store' strategies, such as:

- *loss leader*—a commonly required product that is sold at a very low price to attract people into the store with the aim of selling a 'basket' of other products to make up for the loss

- *bait and switch*—advertising a product at a very low cost but with limited supply that sells out quickly, and then using the opportunity to upsell the customer to a more expensive product

- *anchoring*—discounting from a very high recommended retail price (which the item is never sold for anyway). We often see this in electricity retailing (e.g. 15 per cent off the listed market price)

- *predatory pricing*—this is discounted pricing used to protect your local area from competition. It is often used to hammer a new competitor to stop them getting market share and force them out of business.

Then there are pricing strategies to maximise margins. For example:

- *price skimming*—a new technology, a highly sought-after new product or a scarce product that is sold at a much higher margin to capitalise on the demand

- *house brand*—a brand that you own or have manufactured under exclusively, where the margin can be maximised because it can't be bought elsewhere. By your company taking on the marketing and logistics costs, it reduces the cost for the manufacturer, which they can then pass on

- *price discrimination*—where a different price can be used for different customers, maximising margins where possible. This is more a strategy used at a manufacturing or wholesale level where buying quantities and partner categories are often used as justification for different pricing for different customers.

Make sure you're aware of the different strategies that can be used rather than just pricing all products at the same margin. It's usual to trade off volume for margin. Those products that move quickly, that you can order in higher quantities and that turn over faster reduce costs within your business so they can be sold at lower profit margins. You may also choose to price different categories of products at different margins. A supermarket may choose to sell refrigerated lines that have a higher holding cost or ancillary electrical or pharmacy lines at higher margins than standard grocery items.

Subscription pricing

If you have a software platform that's providing a service, ongoing benefits or a streaming service, a recurring income model that creates a set income over a recurring billing period is a fantastic sales tool. This relies on providing ongoing value, with popular examples being gaming platforms, streaming services (TV, podcasts, etc.) and business accounting and service platforms.

Charging a deposit or pre-payment

To keep a business healthy and your cash flow moving, if there is the opportunity to collect deposits or pre-payment for your product, always do it. Money going out the door paying for products or other overheads before you collect it from selling the product is known as 'negative cash flow' and this must be kept to a minimum by collecting money owed as soon as possible after the product has been sold. If you are collecting your money 30 days after the invoice date or 30 days after end of month, consider offering discount incentives to get this to 14 days or even seven days as it makes an enormous difference to your cash position and ability to pay debts and other overheads faster. You can then use this additional cash reserve to achieve better prices from your suppliers. If you can get yourself into an e-commerce business where you are collecting your money upfront before the expenses are incurred, this is known as a 'positive cash flow' business and it reduces the financial risk enormously. An example of this is where you may have an e-commerce store that takes advantage of a supplier's 'drop-shipping' warehouse. You hold no stock and when you receive an order it gets sent through to the supplier, who fulfils the order, and you receive your payment and profit upfront. It's very difficult in most circumstances to have a fully cash positive business but the aim must be to reduce your negative cash flow as much as possible.

As I always say, timing is everything in business. The ZEN Energy business was built on receiving significant deposits upfront. It was at a time when the technology was new and in demand, the ZEN brand was strong in the market and we placed ourselves in a position where we could scale the business rapidly utilising funding from system deposits that then funded our supply chain.

Service response and exceptional experiences

Let's talk about the rules of engagement: how do we as a business respond to our customers? Will it be immediate? Will it be within a day or longer? How many times will we let the phone ring, how long can people stay on hold and how will we answer the phone? Will the call go directly to the person who can help the customer or will it go through three departments, after which the customer is hung up on? Often, this will depend on the complexity and size of the business, but as a start-up or early-stage scaling business this can be a huge competitive advantage if used correctly. You have the ability to be nimble and react quickly to customer needs so develop your systems around responsiveness and build that into your culture from day one.

Every time the phone rang in any of our companies it had to be answered within three rings by anyone who was available and it had to be answered in the same way: 'Welcome to Regency Food Services. Richard speaking. How can I help you?' The person answering was trained in how to assist the customer. People often act impulsively to purchase a product and these people need to be serviced effectively and quickly so that they feel satisfied they have made the right decision while they are in that frame of mind. This also goes for an e-commerce response: there needs to be an immediate acknowledgement of their presence on the website with an option to get help or, if possible, chat with a real person—or at least a chatbot—with an extensive FAQ list available to answer common questions. If an order is consequently placed, a confirmation must be sent thanking them for their order, together with a receipt and tracking details. From there the physical dispatch and delivery process can really differentiate between companies.

Just this week I was pleasantly surprised and impressed when replacement ink cartridges for my printer appeared on my doorstep the day after I ordered them from an interstate provider. Orders can be batched in your order processing system and, depending on your order volume, can be sent to the warehouse (yours or a third-party warehouse) for stock picking at different intervals during the day. A picking list should be generated in bin location order so one sweep of the warehouse can pick all the stock for that batch and the stock can then be brought into a 'staging' area for individual labelling and dispatch. Dispatching stock to the customer the same day, or at worst the next day, together with confirmed tracking information is always going to be a pleasant surprise. Make sure you have live stock information so people aren't ordering stock that's not available and can't be delivered, not only letting them down but requiring a refund—all of which costs you time, money and most likely a customer.

And the process doesn't end with dispatch. How have you gone about choosing a logistics provider? Have you just chosen the cheapest option to provide to your customer, do you know how long it will take to deliver and could this severely let the customer down if they want the product quickly? I would suggest, where possible, to build an express option into the price of the product (if it's not too much of a cost burden) so you can offer fast, free delivery, which is sure to delight your customers. At a minimum, provide a clear option for express delivery so your customers have a choice if they are impulsive or need a quick delivery, and ensure they are kept informed along the way to build excitement.

The future of physical in-store retail shopping is going to be built on 'experience' shopping and exceptional customer service that simply can't be provided online. The mistake large retailers have been making is cutting back on service and staff to try and compete with online shopping, but this just takes them on a continual downward spiral until they're out of business.

If your brand values and positioning in the market are represented as a low-cost, budget or convenience provider with no expectation of good service in-store, then people are aware of that and they are only there for the price or the convenience. It's when you see high-priced department stores selling luxury goods with extremely poor or non-existent service that you shake your head and think *How long can this last before either online shopping or other quality service-driven outlets take over and these stores are sadly out of business?*

Here's an example of retail shopping being an 'experience'. There's a men's fashion retailer I frequent because I often need help in pairing clothing items and putting an outfit together for an occasion. I have developed a good relationship with the manager, Marc, who through his systems and personal service knows every item he has sold to me and what I have in my wardrobe from his store and will put outfits together with that knowledge, thereby maximising the value I spend on future items. Now that's exceptional customer service that can't be replicated online, and a service I'm prepared to pay a premium for!

That's the future of retail shopping, so don't choose a physical retail store option for your business unless you understand how to differentiate on service and are prepared to go through intensive staff training and role-playing to get a consistently high level of face-to-face service. This is about local knowledge, local service and local ownership in most cases. There are additional overheads in running a retail outlet compared to an online store, or a drop shop that doesn't even have a warehouse, and these have to be balanced out with exceptional customer service and convenience. There's no doubt this is possible, but physical retail has changed, and sloppy, poor, inconsistent service just won't cut it anymore if you want to build a long-term successful business.

If you're a manufacturer or a wholesale business, the same principles of service apply. You still have customers; they're just not at the end of the supply chain. Your customers, whether they be wholesalers or retailers, still have a choice, no matter how much you think you have them locked up. Every company must be in the business of continual improvement because if you aren't, a competitor will emerge and take it away from you. Service response and delivery (fulfilment) is an ever-changing landscape with technology providing ever better ways of communicating with and servicing customers.

When things go wrong

While we're on the subject of rules of engagement with our customers, we also need to acknowledge that things don't always go the way we planned. The way you deal with these situations will separate you as a great company from those that get poor reviews and eventually fall by the wayside. The difference is *communication*. Avoiding a difficult phone call because no-one wants to make the call will only result in an angry customer—and you stand to lose the customer when the entire relationship can easily be salvaged just by explaining what has happened and why. Most customers are reasonable and if there is a valid reason they will usually understand, but timely communication is essential. Don't wait. If the customer is waiting for a crucial delivery or service, the best time to call them is as soon as you find out there's a delay, an issue or that there's a stock out. Give them a chance to source stock elsewhere or help them through the process if you can. If you wait or don't advise them and that delivery just doesn't turn up you have literally thrown yourself and your company under the bus when everything could have been salvaged with a phone call. Also, don't rely on electronic messaging or emails as people are often busy and not always watching their computer or phone. If they're waiting for a delivery and it's not coming, be sure to ring them as soon as you find out.

Service response also relates to the after-sales-service experience, as customers need confidence that if something goes wrong, they're dealing with a trusted business that will support them to ensure their experience meets the brand promise. Rather than anguish over the cost of a replacement for a faulty or damaged product, or a product that just doesn't meet the customer's expectations, a quality business must look beyond this initial cost. Weigh it up against the damage that can be caused by a disgruntled, angry customer who will go out of their way to damage your reputation and put other prospective customers off. This is a much higher cost in the long run than the immediate 'fix' that could have been done to diffuse the issue and preserve the business reputation. Sometimes this is due to the delegation authority that local managers have, or their experience in how to deal with a particular problem, but this is all countered by proper training and culture. This can cause a lot of anxiety for your staff if they can clearly see the issue but aren't allowed to act appropriately to service the customer due to constrictive processes.

Of course, there's always going to be that difficult customer who may try it on for a discount or free stock when everything has actually been done correctly and they were serviced well. In this case you need to be prepared to respond to any public criticism in the same public forum that they used and outline the professional process the customer has been taken through so the public can see the issue is with the customer and not your business.

And finally, there's the process of learning from your customer's experience. It's super important to have good after-sales communication to ensure your customer was satisfied with both the product and the service, and to learn from any negative (or positive) experiences, so negatives can be reduced, and positives enhanced, along with any further suggestions the customer may have. The more personal and open ended this communication is, the better, but it also needs to be quick and efficient so as not to deter the customer from responding. Always aim for ways to improve the response rate so you can learn more on how to further improve your overall business. Some businesses encourage this with a small gift or discount voucher on their next order.

Essentially ...

- Sales is the process of converting an enquiry that comes from your marketing into an actual sale.

- The 'sales channel' that your customer comes to *must* be consistent with the brand and brand values portrayed in your marketing material (website/retail store/salesperson) or your business will fail to convert a significant percentage of enquiries into sales.

- Presentation must be professional, clear and functional. It must be designed to trigger that 'emotive' purchase response flowing from your marketing material.

- Numerous pricing techniques can be used to inspire customers to purchase. Appropriate delegation of authority may be given to sales staff to negotiate in certain circumstances.

- Recurring income through subscription pricing is a great model if achievable, but requires continual content value for the customer.

- Reduce any negative cash flow in the business to a minimum by using incentives on payment terms for customers to pay faster or by taking deposits on orders.

- Service response must be exceptional and clear procedures and processes must be in place on how to engage with customers to provide exceptional service and consistency each time they purchase.

- Build in express delivery where possible so free, fast delivery can be promoted or, depending on the type of business, the fastest practical and responsive service that can be provided with full tracking. You could even GPS track for distribution services to retail or wholesale businesses so they can plan to receive the stock.

- After-sales feedback, learning and continual improvement is essential in your business to stay ahead of your competition and to take advantage of new technology as it emerges.

CHAPTER 8

Sourcing suppliers and manufacturing

During the 1900s, and certainly up to the 1980s, there was a strong drive towards local, or 'sovereign', manufacturing driven by Australia's determination to become an independent and self-sufficient nation. And developing nations were just that—developing.

Over the past 40 years, however, there has been a continuing trend to seek lower cost manufacturing overseas as those developing nations started to mature and stabilise, and with large populations of very low cost labour available they could develop a manufacturing base that provided a significant cost advantage over local manufacturing. As a result, we saw numerous industry sectors heading overseas for supply.

Over the past 20 years, though, we have been confronted with scenes of manufacturing 'sweat shops'—utilising what we would deem slave labour—that deeply shocked the general community. This in itself has resulted in a manufacturing movement by companies towards ethically sourced products in response to market demand. Not all products can be sourced and manufactured successfully, whether it be in Australia or other developed nations; however, effort can be put into ensuring our values and quality control processes are maintained within those supply chains in other countries.

The COVID-19 pandemic raised other critical issues with overseas supply due to volatile movements in demand and populations being locked down. This saw a huge reduction in available supply from manufacturers together with international freight channels being heavily restricted and quarantine measures being put in place. As a result, both lead times for stock and costs went through the roof causing major supply, pricing and cash-flow issues for companies.

So you need to make a decision on where to source your products from. Do you look overseas and question whether supply will return to something like 'normal' in the near future, or do you start the process of looking for faster, more reliable local manufacturers? Having dealt with both, I've seen the pros and cons of each and I'll share some of them with you now.

Local sourcing

It's certainly an advantage to share the same culture with a business partner when you're negotiating and managing expectations, particularly for new business owners who haven't had the experience of dealing with other cultures. Detailed information being lost in translation is a real issue so it's important to put in place systems to ensure expectations are met and negotiations are understood.

Sourcing locally supports local jobs and, in turn, the local economy, and should provide fast access to the finished product by avoiding international supply chains and potentially volatile cost rises in freight, particularly if you're relying on shipping channels. (The cost of booking shipping containers rose by a factor of 10 in 2021, causing major cost issues in relation to landed freight.) You're also not subject to geopolitical issues, which could interrupt your supply chain and export access to a major customer market, as we've seen in recent times in Australia. And you'll want to make sure your local manufacturers aren't reliant on overseas supply for components either.

Energy costs (from the rapid rollout of renewables), together with manufacturing automation and other input costs, have been coming down in Australia while overseas manufacturing has seen many cost increases so the disparity in costs are certainly not what they used to be.

I would strongly recommend you do your research and look for a local manufacturing partner in the first instance, if that opportunity exists for you. There's certainly a shift in consumer sentiment that can be brought into your marketing plan to reflect your local sourcing strategy, a low emissions supply chain and the local partnerships you form to benefit the home economy.

International sourcing

If you still feel an overseas supplier is the best source for your product supply, then here are a few of my tips for finding the right one.

Firstly, how do you find them? In days gone by you simply had no choice but to get over to those countries, visit the factories, see who had the capabilities and do your best on the negotiations. Over time, you'd invest in building a relationship that worked and was trusted, which also created significant value in your business.

These days finding potential suppliers is much easier with search engines such as Alibaba, AliExpress, Global Sources and many others. However, there is still the issue of understanding their capabilities and where they sit in the market.

If you look for a supplier on Alibaba, for instance, chances are 10 suppliers of a product will show up. They usually all look similar and they even share the same images in many cases, which makes things really confusing! Are they all the manufacturer of the product? The short answer is 'no'. What you'll find is many agents of the one manufacturer representing themselves as the manufacturer and all taking a margin reselling the same thing. So you need to ask them some very direct questions about their manufacturing capabilities, ability to modify the product and minimum order quantities. In order to understand who is the real manufacturer, ultimately you may have to get on a plane and do your own due diligence by seeing first-hand who they are and their capabilities.

Before you go to that expense, it's certainly worthwhile testing product samples from various suppliers. Test their ability to manufacture your product without giving away too much of the final design, or alter their standard product to encompass some of your specifications, and test their ability to manufacture under your brand. Make sure you have an NDA in place, or better still a trademark or provisional patent over your brand and technology if relevant. Good ideas will quickly be copied in other countries if they're not properly protected or at least represented to the supplier as having protection in place.

When communicating with them, it's a good idea to spend time reinforcing your longer term manufacturing partnership objectives because they will see your order of samples as simply another order, not as a way of testing out their capabilities. Once you start to home in on who you deem to be the right manufacturer, you really need to then focus on developing your relationship. International suppliers value a personal visit highly as it demonstrates your willingness to work with them. They will want to take you on a factory tour and show off all their capabilities. Make sure you go out for dinner and a celebratory drink as this is also valued highly and builds on the personal relationship and mutual respect of both businesses.

I clearly remember searching for my first solar panel manufacturer, and after sourcing a German manufacturer for the critically important electronics within the ZEN inverters, I found a high-quality Asian manufacturer for the panels primarily to provide a shorter lead time into Australia for what was going to be a high-volume line. There were no manufacturing options in Australia with the capability we were after. I found a company that I was reasonably confident in. They had started the same year we started and at that time had just one manual production line, but they were very proud of their quality and processes.

We were all bluff and bravado at the time, as you need to be when starting a company, and represented ourselves as the next big thing in the emerging renewables sector in Australia. Even though we barely had a business, we did have a solid business plan and brand. When we arrived at the company's offices in Taizhou, China, the entire staff was out the front singing the company song! We couldn't believe our eyes (or ears) and wondered how we would pull this off! It turned out my wife and I unknowingly had a powerful weapon with us: our three-month-old baby girl. Little did we know that our little girl from Australia would be a symbol of good fortune. Everyone wanted to admire and have their photo taken with her, including the CEO and chairman, which immediately opened the doors to a very fruitful and entertaining relationship.

We had dinner together each night we were there, and we ate and drank far too much, with many rounds of 'Cheers'—or 'Gānbēi', as they say in China, which literally means 'dry cup'—and, unlike in the West, you're expected to empty your glass after each toast, or at least give it your best shot! No-one was in the best of form the next morning, but at that time it was essential to build a strong relationship with trust and a deeper understanding of each other's needs.

We toured the factory and the manufacturing facility to see examples of finished products and discuss quality expectations, finishes, packaging and branding options. Our visit also provided the opportunity to talk about quality control processes, continuous improvement cycles and how they proposed to protect our brand and other intellectual property.

Warranties

A discussion needs to be had early on around defective products and how warranties will be managed. Culturally these can be seen differently, and you have to meet your obligations to your own country's legal requirements and also to your own company's promise to your customers.

It's difficult and expensive to send faulty products back to an overseas supplier. A clear process has to be negotiated detailing, for example, what information and images the manufacturer will accept as proof of a faulty product so that you can replace the goods from your local stock holding and service the customer immediately without tedious delays. The same goes if a full refund is required: a credit against the supplier's account must be a trusted and acknowledged process. This can quickly become an area of tension if it's not clearly negotiated upfront.

Minimum order quantities (MOQs)

Another challenging area in dealing with overseas supply is negotiating minimum order quantities (MOQs). In my experience, a new supplier will always push for container quantities or at least significant volumes upfront as the MOQ, which causes a lot of stress for a start-up or early-stage business. This, of course, works best for the supplier and is a great excuse to force a large order onto a naive customer. However, from your point of view there's huge risk in undertaking an order of that size—which could be in the tens of thousands or even hundreds of thousands of dollars in value—first up.

My advice is, quite simply, *Don't do it!* Bring in the bluff. Let them know you're building a large business, you need to test their capability to supply and the quality of their product and packaging over a series of much smaller orders at the best price, and that you'll eventually get to the order size they want. What you are really doing is creating the opportunity to take smaller quantities, and hopefully pre-selling or selling them quickly to build cash flow and profits, enabling you to buy a slightly larger quantity next time and to keep your word. Building a business is a two-way street of 'give and take' with suppliers. They will be relentless in trying to force you into taking larger quantities quickly. But keep to your plan and push them hard on the smaller quantities to build your business in manageable steps.

Freight forwarding

To arrange air or sea freight of your commercial product into your country you'll need to engage a freight forwarder, who will arrange collection of the goods from the factory, load them onto the vessel, and organise the shipping and customs paperwork—including the 'bill of lading', which is generally the trigger for payment. When dealing with overseas suppliers you'll be expected to pay upfront for your goods when the ship is loaded. This means you won't have goods to sell or cash flow while the shipment is in transit, so make sure you work this into your budget. This is a major implication when dealing with overseas suppliers, particularly when dealing with European suppliers, because stock may be on the water for six weeks or more.

The freight forwarder will also manage customs and tax paperwork when the goods enter the country of destination. At this point, you'll have to pay the GST (or sales tax) upfront before you collect it on sales, which can also contribute to a significant negative cash flow.

Account terms

In time, once your relationship with the supplier has settled and trust is flowing both ways, the conversation can turn to account terms, where your aim should initially be to negate the time the stock is on the water.

Depending on the country of the manufacturer, they will sometimes negotiate credit insurance under arrangement or backing by the government, or separately negotiate terms with their bank that they can pass on to you.

If supply is out of Asia, start by trying to negotiate 30 days from bill of lading, or if supply is out of Europe or the United States, try to negotiate 60 days from bill of lading. It made an incredible difference to our company shifting a good part of the risk back to the supplier, and gave us leverage to push for even better pricing to grow the market faster so we both benefited from the arrangements.

Shipping times and delays

Generally, shipping times from Asia are two to three weeks to Australia, depending on which ports are involved. From the United States it's between four and six weeks and from Europe it can be more than six weeks. Talk to your freight forwarder about the route to be taken and whether there will be 'cross-docking', where your shipment may change ships at a port such as Singapore, which happens at certain times of the year. In the first six months of the year this may not affect transit times much at all and may provide more flexibility to access vessels. However, in the six months leading up to Christmas, when shipping lanes are congested, I've had experiences where a shipment can literally sit on a cross-dock for three weeks waiting to be collected, causing untold dramas for customers waiting for their stock.

During these times of the year, it's worth trying to negotiate a direct shipment without cross-docking to have a much better chance of deliveries arriving on time, even if it costs a bit more for the convenience.

Drop shipping

A relatively new alternative to managing stock has been the evolution of drop shipping, where your customers' orders are fed directly through to the manufacturer or their warehouse online for direct dispatch to the customer. You are surrendering some control over your business but gaining a number of advantages including a positive cash flow, because you're being paid immediately on a professional payment platform before the shipment has even been made, and you have professional warehousing for live stock control and immediate dispatch, including full tracking services. This is a great solution for centralised global shipping but delivery could take a while compared to local services, particularly during a pandemic, and express options can be costly on small quantities internationally.

Services such as Amazon, and other online marketplaces, including industry-specific options now evolving, have grown extensively on the back of drop shipping, enabling online retailers to set up their stores on the Amazon platform and benefit from its entire suite of integrated backend logistics services.

Essentially...

- There is a big shift back to local sovereign supply and manufacturing to avoid the rising cost and unpredictable externalities that can affect international manufacturers and freight. There is always the potential for an international crisis or pandemic, so consider local supply chains in the first instance — after all, it's good for our local economy and jobs.

- If you feel the need to go international, there are sourcing platforms available that find manufacturers in various countries, but you will need to filter through those representing themselves as manufacturers to find the ones that actually are manufacturers with the right capabilities.

- Approach the relationship with suppliers confidently when you're negotiating samples and minimum order quantities and hint at a bigger relationship if they can look after you with smaller early orders. Don't be bullied into purchasing full containers straight away.

- To build the relationship, it's always an important step to physically visit the factory, if you can, to establish a personal relationship and discuss design, quality, branding and the protection of your intellectual property.

(continued)

- There are cultural differences in the way warranties are perceived and managed, so clear processes need to be established before significant trade starts to ensure you're not left holding defective stock.

- Engage a freight forwarder to manage your freight from the manufacturer to your door. They will take care of the customs, shipping and tax paperwork.

- Money for stock will be due when the ship leaves your supplier's port. As you build your international supplier relationship, work on ways to negotiate account terms for payments to negate the time your stock is on the water and the resulting cash-flow implications.

- Find out if drop shipping is an option for your business, particularly if your business is online retail, not forgetting that there are some disadvantages to this.

CHAPTER 9

Innovation, re-invention and disruption

Being successful begins with looking for ways to change the way an industry operates. Without that you're just competing against established businesses on their playing field.

They already have the financial backing, customers, infrastructure, people and processes to defend their market share and will make it very difficult for you to compete as a start-up, unless you change the way the industry operates and make it difficult for them to manoeuvre and compete.

If you're smart enough and nimble enough, you can literally use their market strength as a weakness, leveraging their inability to quickly change their business model to counter your new approach. Let me share some strategies I've used to gain a market advantage and accelerate growth in my own businesses.

Aligning to your customer

In our first business, Regency Food Services, my brother Greg and I realised that our business was operating as traditional distribution warehouses did, from early morning until mid-afternoon, yet the market we were servicing, being hospitality, was operating from lunchtime until late evening—almost opposite hours of the clock!

As a result, orders were largely left on answering machines well after our sales staff had gone home. Chefs, who generally ordered their nightly (large) orders to replenish the kitchen after their dinner service, were often tired and short tempered and didn't provide the best descriptions, and then weren't available if we wanted to clarify their order in the morning. 'Send me the usual brand I have' or 'you know what I want' were among the vague descriptions given, resulting in wrong orders and expensive couriers, and of course it's difficult to push customers to accept liability for any mistakes.

We came to the realisation that if we were going to service the hospitality industry successfully, we had to work the same hours they worked and actually talk to them with empathy and a focus on service.

We quickly set about creating the first 24-hour food service distribution operation in Australia, negotiating a key enterprise bargaining agreement (EBA) with our staff to enable them to work overnight.

We then recruited and trained tele-sales staff to work in three shifts, so we had staff available until 10 pm to call our customers for their orders after their dinner trade, enabling them to talk through and confirm every line. Next we pushed the bleeding edge of the technology of the day to process batch-picking sheets for our warehouse from 10 pm to midnight, batch-picked the stock, with one sweep of the warehouse done for each truck, and then staged (prepared and sorted the stock) into reverse delivery order and loaded our trucks, using large telescopic loaders, enabling them to be on the road by 4 am.

This process provided a number of strategic market advantages to our company, including a significantly reduced number of costly errors. We were the last to take personalised orders in the evening and the first on the road to deliver the next day. On the back of this initiative the company grew very quickly and I clearly remember the call from the CEO of Qantas Flight Catering in January 1996 when we were awarded the food service supply contract for Qantas in South Australia, followed closely by another contract for the huge Olympic Dam mining operation soon after.

Think laterally

Another innovation was when the company laterally extended into hospitality staffing in 1996 with the creation of Regency Staffing. It was at a time when cafés were exploding across the hospitality scene and good staff, both front and back of house, were short in supply. Our food sales team were often being asked to sound out staff in other venues in a crude attempt by hospitality managers to try and poach staff if possible.

It became evident that an opportunity existed to establish a small hospitality staffing operation to assist in this area for an appropriate service fee, so we started putting our thoughts into developing a business even though we had no immediate experience in the field.

We spoke to a senior recruitment consultant, who was helping our business with our own recruitment at the time about the concept, and she agreed the opportunity was there and was willing to set up and operate the business for us. We developed a business plan and in no time Regency Staffing was underway and within a year had surpassed $1 million in revenue!

Not only was the service a benefit to our existing customers, but it also helped recruit many new customers to both businesses. In addition to the recruitment service itself, we also provided a labour hire service and a flexible workforce for many establishments that were experiencing changes in demand throughout the year. This enabled us to literally be the employer of hundreds of chefs and food and beverage staff who were placed in many large and progressive venues including Qantas flight catering.

A further 'circular' benefit from employing the chefs, in particular, who in most cases ordered the food, was their support for Regency Staffing and Regency Food Services for getting them jobs in these venues. So, in most cases, we were the immediate first choice for the venue's food supply. A very entrepreneurial outcome for our business resulting in the combined companies being awarded the 1996 Ernst and Young Entrepreneur of the Year award for South Australia.

Be ahead of the game

My most recent business, ZEN Energy, landed in the incredibly challenging arena of pioneering the renewable energy industry in Australia. This was a market governed by very complex rules and regulations designed for fossil fuel generators and retailers together with incumbent operators, who were heavily vested in a very controlled market and were not prepared to let new technology entrants join in a hurry.

As ZEN transitioned from a solar energy business to incorporate leading energy storage technologies and later becoming a full energy generator and retailer, it was quickly heading into an area beyond my personal knowledge and experience. It became clear I was going to need to bring experts into the business to navigate this complex journey if the company was going to reach its full potential.

We needed the energy density that Li-ion battery storage technology promised with the application of the technology from residential to grid scale. This would be the enabler for large-scale renewables connected to the grid, balancing both voltage and frequency from the intermittent generation of solar and wind. Access to this technology came to us through our first investment by Raymond Spencer, a remarkable Australian entrepreneur, who was introduced to ZEN Energy as chair of the judging panel for the Ernst & Young Australian Entrepreneur of the Year award in 2010 when ZEN Energy won the Cleantech sector.

Raymond was also an early director of Greensmith Energy Management in the United States, which was pioneering grid-scale energy storage at a global level. This formal connection with Greensmith placed ZEN five years ahead of the market in Australia, enabling us to build a strong profile as the leaders in grid-scale energy storage in Australia with Raymond as chairman of our first formal board in 2010.

We leveraged the PR and media from this opportunity, but many regulatory hurdles made the progression and entry of grid-scale batteries into the Australian grid a very slow and painful exercise, and it was clear we needed influence to progress these required regulatory changes.

In 2015, Professor Ross Garnaut—Australia's pre-eminent economics professor from the University of Melbourne, who was commissioned to undertake the 2008 and 2011 Garnaut Climate Change Review into the economic impact of climate change in Australia—decided it was time to play an active role in the transition of our energy system to renewables. Professor Garnaut had projected the severe impact that climate change was going to have and had developed a number of progressive initiatives for the federal government, but by 2015 he wanted to become actively involved and was looking for an opportunity to partner with the right people and technology to effect real change. This is when he was introduced to ZEN Energy.

The fit was right. ZEN needed the market influence that Ross could provide and together he and the company were able to commence its transition to an energy generator and retailer. Ross invested and became chairman and Raymond continued as deputy chair. The company was developing a formidable board and management team.

The next key piece to the jigsaw in rolling out large-scale renewable projects, including solar farms, wind farms and big batteries, was to have a key customer take the power and de-risk the huge financial outlay. For ZEN this came in the form of GFG Alliance—with Sanjeev Gupta as its executive chairman—and its investment into Liberty Steel and its associated businesses across Australia.

The model GFG used in the UK to revive the traditional steel industry was to deploy large-scale renewables to significantly reduce the cost of electricity to their operations including hydro, wind, tidal and batteries. GFG made significant and successful investments in the renewable energy supply chain and had to do the same in Australia, recognising that when solar was added to that mix the cost reductions would be even higher, making the business in Australia globally competitive.

While negotiations were underway to acquire the steelworks, parallel talks were already in place with ZEN to put our companies together and replicate the UK model, as we had the people, technology and influence, and there was no point re-inventing the wheel.

In October 2017, ZEN Energy embarked on a merger with Sanjeev Gupta's global GFG Alliance, which acquired a 50.1 per cent majority shareholding in the company and rebranded itself as SIMEC Energy Australia to fit GFG's global branding. It retained the ZEN Energy brand for its traditional residential and commercial businesses. The company's vision was to create Australia's first major clean energy generator, consumer and retailer—to not only supply GFG's heavy energy-consuming steel and resource businesses with globally competitive clean electricity, but to build out enough generation to supply a significant segment of industrial and commercial Australia to meet the ambitions of the ZEN Energy board and to become Australia's first major clean energy retailer.

Unfortunately, though, not all best-laid plans go exactly the way they were intended and re-invention was yet again necessary and strategically planned.

In early 2020, due to delays in the construction of key projects on the GFG side, the ZEN board moved towards a demerger with GFG, enabling ZEN to move forward independently with its plan to become one of Australia's largest clean energy electricity retailers and to work towards becoming a full clean energy utility. This demerger was completed in September 2020 and the company is now one of the largest electricity retailers in Australia with its clean energy generating assets spread across the country. ZEN Energy has *reset* its business following the theme established by Professor Ross Garnaut's latest book, *Reset*, and its solar and battery business still leads the residential and commercial markets, and is fully integrated with its electricity retailing business.

This was a complex and disruptive journey that needed strategic investment by key people to be successful by re-inventing a company to now become a significant 'new energy' electricity retailer in Australia.

It's a great example of identifying early on what journey you're going on, how you're going to disrupt a market and whether you have the skills to complete that journey—and if not, what skills and people you need to bring on board.

Flavia on innovation

Flavia has been relentless in her focus of changing the economics of managing both technology and communications from space. She talks about how this has been a game changer not only for her business, but also because it opens up so many more opportunities for new applications.

A constellation of small satellites changes the economics of providing communication services from space. Space infrastructure has always been so expensive, but suddenly it's becoming more affordable and now opens itself up to a lot of high-quality applications that in the past would never have used satellite data.

It's like the super computers from the time of the Apollo missions (which in reality had less computing power than a modern-day iPhone), which were only available in universities and within government. Suddenly you build the iPhone and everyone has one... and once everyone has one the opportunity for building lots of applications is amazing!

Haigh's third-generation innovation

Claude's son John completed school in 1945 and joined the company the following year, starting in the factory and, over time, learning all aspects of the business operation. Innovation started to gain pace in this period and during the late 1940s work was done to the Haigh's factory to ramp up the production of Easter eggs to commence supply to supermarkets. This was a fruitful investment that paid for the machinery in the first year and allowed them to beat the supermarkets at their own game. It placed Haigh's in a very strong negotiating position as the supermarkets would continually try to push prices down in the hope the manufacturer needed the volume to pay off the machinery and service the bank debt and would just accept the reduced price — a tactic they still use today with both food and wine manufacturers alike. Today Haigh's has about seventy product lines that come in only for Easter.

At the time, John Haigh wanted to further improve the quality of chocolate making so he went to Switzerland and was fortunate to get a job at Lindt chocolates where he learned the craft of making fine chocolate. He took note of the supply chains that were the quality bean suppliers and the different bean varieties being used, and on his return to Australia was able to secure supply for Haigh's.

John also travelled to the United States after his time at Lindt to see how the biggest brands in the confectionery sector designed and set up their retail operations and undertook their marketing. John also studied their manufacturing processes to bring more sophistication to the overall business. Europe had the traditional chocolatiers but they weren't designed to operate like the chains that were building up in the United States. John came back to Australia, bringing together the best of both worlds, and set up the Haigh's chocolate manufacturing room utilising European machinery, moving to a five-roll refining process which was state of the art at the time and very much still is.

John Haigh is credited with transforming the company into the quality manufacturer that it is today: a very different company from the 1930s and 1940s where they were dealing with sugar rations and other shortages during the Depression years and making chocolate for the armed forces during the war. When picture theatres grew in popularity postwar, Haigh's took advantage of the developing market and rolled out about 25 theatre stores, which was a big driver of growth through that period.

Simon says a key sustainable advantage for Haigh's over the years that has maintained their leadership in the premium chocolate category is that they still make their own chocolate, managing it from bean through to the customer, controlling the product from day one of the process. They don't go out to wholesalers. If there's feedback from the customer, it goes full circle within the business and is reported back to the customer. One of the systems Haigh's has upgraded recently is their customer service portal: it now has quick response times and is fully quantifiable to customers. Haigh's has even appointed a dedicated customer experience manager to manage this system and to reinforce their quality approach.

Haigh's, like many others, ramped up their online shopping portal very quickly during the COVID-19 pandemic, squeezing what they thought would be five years' work into six months! Were all the systems in place to do that? Simon answers, 'No, of course not! Just like no-one else's were', and it was Easter 2020, so they were fully stocked and had to utilise all available options to sell.

Essentially...

- Don't design a business to merely compete against existing businesses because they are already established, which gives them a strong market advantage.

- Ask yourself how you're going to change the way an industry currently operates with both your product and service.

- Leverage the inability of large, established players to quickly change the way they operate and use that to your advantage.

CHAPTER 10
Defining a new market

If you're going to disrupt or re-invent an industry, I recommend you give it a new name and launch that name through strategic PR, positioning you and your company as the leader of that new industry, like we did with ZEN.

Instead of becoming a solar company, we created a whole new market category for ZEN—'home energy'—and called the company ZEN Home Energy Systems. In doing so, we became the self-proclaimed leaders of this exciting new market category. I sat down with the manager of my PR company to create media stories around the topic of home energy and I became the person all the journalists would go to for comment—and by default, this positioned me as the home energy 'expert'!

We then used this as the platform to build the profile of the ZEN range of solar home energy systems. My goal was to build confidence in the brand, as the technology was very new at the time and still very much in the realm of 'weird science' for most people—so faith in the brand was going to be critical.

We reviewed manufacturers from around the world and pieced together who we deemed to be the best component manufacturers in the space at the time, settling on companies from both Germany and China. The challenge was to get them to agree to manufacture under our brand

and to integrate the components into a system format, and there were certainly challenges in getting these culturally different countries to work together!

We needed to take what was fundamentally quite a complex product to market in an easy-to-understand format, so we developed four sizes of the ZEN home energy system that would power from one-quarter of the average home to all of the average home. We took care of the system quality and matching of components. All the customer had to do was trust the brand and quality standard we had set and then choose the system size that met their needs and budget.

The result was that we literally pioneered the modern solar industry in Australia. The company created an extremely 'hot' market in an environment that was primed for a product that promised home energy independence. We gave the consumer confidence in the product, which, when paired with a high level of service, enabled us to position ourselves as a premium Australian technology brand.

Following on from the rapid awareness we had created in the home energy category, tenders started coming out for 'home energy systems'. No prize for guessing who won those tenders and who people turned to for comment! It's far more strategic to lead than to follow, so if you're disrupting an industry model, give it a new name, get on the front foot and lead the market.

And, as we saw in chapter 6, once your company is established, a key role of your PR agent is to work closely with media outlets to bring to your attention upcoming stories on the sector you're targeting so you can participate. This also allows for stories to be written where you have the opportunity to feature as the 'industry expert' for journalists to draw comment from. I was given the opportunity to be involved in the story and provide my 'expert' commentary on anything to do with energy in the home. The journalist would then bring the conversation back to our 'new sector' name and our products.

Essentially...

- Where possible, create a new market category or sector name for your product or service so you can become the leader of that new sector.

- It's better to lead on the front foot when innovating or disrupting a market than to follow.

- It's better for other people to be talking about you than you talking about yourself, so utilise PR companies to build your profile.

CHAPTER 11

Getting investment ready

Apart from equity and ownership questions, which I'll address in the next chapter, questions around getting ready for investment are the most frequent questions I'm asked—and understandably so, as most people don't have the funds available to get started and turn their business ideas into reality.

Let's begin by defining the different stages of developing a new business, the normal pathway of development and in general what funds are required. You'll hear terms such as 'start-up', 'accelerator', 'scale-up', 'growth' and sometimes a combination of these. People use different definitions, which can be very confusing when you're trying to work out what to do. For this reason, I'm going right back to the basics.

Stage 1: Start-up

Stage 1 is the start-up stage. This represents the incubation stage of a new business. It's taking the idea and turning it into something that can be tested or validated; developing a minimum viable product (MVP) or mock-ups that can be demonstrated; and testing it via market research to see whether it's solving a real problem, whether the timing is right and what people will pay for it. Once you're confident you're on the right track and the product design and market acceptance are good, it's then about getting engagement with a real commercial customer or group of consumers so you're ready to run a significant trial or pilot. You've de-risked the business model and have an engaging investor presentation ready to pitch.

The time and money it will take to manage this start-up stage will be different for every business. Some may take very little time and money, while others could take a significant amount of both. On average, for a serious commercial start-up, you'll need to allow up to a couple of years and the 'pre-seed' money you would be looking to raise is generally in the vicinity of AUD$100000 to $500000. Some people will use their own savings. If there are two or three founders, it becomes a bit easier as you'll probably share the burden. As we saw in chapter 2, choosing to fund the start-up with your own money is called 'bootstrapping'. Founders will often still be working their day jobs either full time or part time to keep the required funding flowing during stage 1 while working after hours on their venture, and will then progressively wind back their day job hours as the business becomes more real and ready to launch into a commercial paid trial.

Finding investors

If bootstrapping is out of the question, or you simply don't want to take that risk with your own money, then it has to come from somewhere else. As I mentioned in chapter 2, most people start with the three Fs: family, friends and fools. These are people who believe in you, think you are onto something and want to see you have a go in a low financial risk environment.

This money could be in the form of a gift (if you're very lucky), a loan or maybe you'll grant them a share of your business in return for the money. At this stage it's purely a discussion on what percentage you're willing to offer in exchange for their money as the business isn't proven. It's really a gamble on both sides and should only involve money they can afford to lose if things go awry.

If family or friends are not an option, you could look for what's known as an 'angel investor'. This is usually someone who has built a business previously, has had the experience of growing a business and exited, and is now keen to invest and help others for a measured return. This person may act independently or be part of an angel investing group or network. A key question to ask yourself at this stage is *What type of person do you want?* Do you want the person to be a silent investor who only contributes money—known as 'dumb money'—or do you want someone who can add real value to your business in terms of contacts, networks, technology or skills that can help fast-track your development? If the latter is the case, you need to spend time getting to know the person first, and ensure you're absolutely compatible and that the investor shares your passion. This is known as 'smart money'.

Angel investor networks can be found on the internet or through your research, or you may have found a couple of key industry people you would like to target as early investors. Either way, you'll need to entice them to hear your presentation pitch. Maybe you can plan this through an introduction, which is the best way, so that you have time to present in detail. Sometimes it can be more strategic: you might 'bump' into them in the elevator where you have a couple of minutes to quickly engage, get their attention and hopefully score a chance to meet them later to discuss your opportunity in more detail. This is where the term 'elevator pitch' comes from. Professional online networks such as LinkedIn offer an easier, though less personal, way to connect—but you'll still need that elevator pitch!

Pitching your idea

Pitching or professionally presenting your business and its strategy is critical at all stages of the business—gaining investors, reporting to bankers, selling to customers, impressing suppliers to get favourable terms and a market advantage—so you need to get used to talking about yourself and the business in a professional and engaging way. Doing a short course in public speaking is a good idea if you haven't had that experience or if you're an introvert by nature.

So what's covered in a good investor presentation and how long should it go for? It has to be impactful—in fact, hard hitting enough to smack you between the eyes in a 'no brainer' kind of way—and you should prepare a 10- and a 20-minute version. A good graphic designer with a marketing brain is always helpful for creating the necessary impact. To be taken seriously, the presentation must look professional and credible because a potential investor will be using this to gauge your ability to run a well-crafted, fast-growth business.

The content for an investor presentation deck needs to include the following:

- *What the problem is you're solving and why the timing is right.* Present it as a day-to-day frustration that people can easily relate to in their own lives.

- *Market opportunity.* The size of the market globally/regionally in dollars and the percentage of that market you're targeting with your product.

- *An introduction to your product and brand.* Explain to potential stakeholders clearly what makes your product different from anything else on the market, identifying competitors and the advantage you have over them.

- *Whether you're disrupting or re-inventing a market.* Explain clearly how you are changing the industry model and the sustainable advantage this will give you over your competitors.

- *Intellectual property protection.* Do you have a trademark or patent over your brand, invention/technology or methodology? Is it in process or secured? Also be aware that coders of websites or software and designers have automatic copyright of their work so you need to ensure that the person coding or designing has 'assigned' or transferred their ownership of the copyright to you. If they don't, it can be problematic down the track as you expand. (You can read more about this in chapter 13.)

- *What your go-to-market plan is.* How are you going to reach your market and communicate your marketing plan to create demand and enquiries? What is your sales strategy (how will you convert enquiries to sales)? What operational/management experience does your team have to successfully manage and deliver your product or service to the market, obtain feedback and continually improve your offering to maintain your point of difference and stay ahead of the market?

- *Your growth, revenue and profit forecasts for the first three years.* When will you break even (stop any cash burn)?

- *Your investment needs.* What is your ask? How much money do you need, how will it be used and what percentage of the company are you willing to give in return? What was the basis for your current valuation of the business? The investor will fundamentally want to know how you are going to use their money to add value to the business and provide them with a significant return on their funds in return for the risk they are taking.

- *Investor support.* What involvement or support are you looking for from the investors to enable the business plan beyond the funding (remember smart money vs dumb money)?

- *Your exit plan.* How are you going to get out of the business and realise the value you have created for yourself and any investors? Who would buy it and how would you target them for a future sale?

You must demonstrate excitement and passion for your business and know the numbers inside out so that potential investors come away convinced of your plan.

Remember, the more you can prove a business model in the marketplace before raising capital, the lower the risk for the investor and the less equity (percentage of ownership) you will need to give away in return for the investment.

The 'pre-seed' money is what you use to get your business ready for a significant commercial trial to prove your business model. This also graduates you into stage 2 of the process, which is the scale-up phase. To run a significant commercial trial and successfully commercialise your business will, in most cases, take a serious amount of additional money and time. This round of fundraising is generally known as the 'seed round', and again the amount required varies significantly from business to business and depending on the speed at which you're growing, but in general can range from AUD$500000 to $5 million.

Stage 2: Scale-up

Scale-up is the most critical phase of a company and is where most companies fail. This is discussed in detail in chapter 16.

Once you have proven your business model in the market with a significant commercial trial, it is critical to get people talking about it in the media and to garner the attention of potential investors. There is so much hype around today about pitch events, which to me is more about reality TV and entertainment than actually getting the right investors on board for success. It's always vital to have a pitch ready for when an opportunity arises, whether it's the two-minute elevator pitch or the 10- to 20-minute slide deck presentation.

The best investor is always the one who finds you! They're likely to already be sold on your business. They may have heard about it through the media, success stories, awards or personal recommendation. If this is the case, the negotiating terms are already on your side if you present a convincing and well-thought-out plan.

Personally, I've never pitched at an event as the right investors always found us. Part of your job as a start-up entrepreneur is creating the right level of positive exposure at the right time when you need it—again, timing is everything!

Venture capital (VC) market overview

Kirsten Bernhardt from Artesian Ventures puts her investor lens on for us to understand what investors and VCs really want.

Before joining Artesian Ventures, Kirsten spent time in the United States and was actively involved in the seed stage fundraising community. She says the market is definitely very active in Australia with a number of funds that have been around more than 10 years. Several funds are now able to demonstrate success to their investors, and raise very large funds (Blackbird is an example of this).

Kirsten says it's nice to see the emergence of new sector-specific funds, which she believes will continue to evolve. She explains:

> It means if you're an early-stage company in Australia, you're not just going to a generic list of VC funds. If you're a SAAS (software as a service) company, for example, you will have specific investors that really understand your business; or if you're an impact driven company there is a list of impact focused investors that will closely align with your values; and so on.

This is an evolution that shows the maturity of the VC market in Australia. However, in Australia the limited partners (LPs)—these are the ones who provide the capital to their funds and the fund managers to invest—are still largely superannuation funds, and that comes with its own responsibilities as only a small percentage of superannuation money can go into VC funds due to their asset risk allocations.

The challenge now is not so much 'more money', but more LPs to get more diversity into the market alongside superannuation funds. Kirsten says she has seen an increase in overseas capital coming into Australia in recent years, and she believes we need to ensure there is enough VC money in Australia to provide access to capital for great companies across all stages of their lifecycle. It's now a matter of increasing the number of LPs (including offshore investors, family offices and the private wealth community) to grow the total funds under management in Australian VC.

(continued)

Artesian Ventures: the largest VC in Australia by portfolio

Artesian is an alternative asset manager specialising in venture capital and debt investments. Artesian's venture business, Artesian Venture Partners (AVP) has screened over 10,000 deals since 2012 and has a portfolio of >650 early-stage ventures (pre-seed to Series A) across Australia and the broader Asia Pacific region, representing assests under management of nearly $600 million.

AVP is one of the region's largest and most active early-stage investors, making 100 to 120 early-stage investments annually. It provides financial and strategic access for institutional investors, government organisations, industry groups, corporations and family offices into the early-stage innovation ecosystem in Australia/NZ and the Asia Pacific region. AVP specialises in critical technology sectors including climate and clean energy, agriculture and food security, health and well-being, AI and robotics, education, and gender equality.

AVP can both lead and follow on in rounds. Leading a round can be important for an investor because they get to set the terms and price the deal, and typically contribute the largest amount of capital to the transaction.

What characteristics do investors and VCs look for in a founding entrepreneur?

To have high conviction in early-stage investing, the 'founding team' is the #1 priority VCs will look at. Those who have done it before have had experience, so a second-time founder is great, and they don't have to necessarily have been successful the first time around as failures often teach you as much as success does. If you've gone through the process of starting a business, raising capital, building a product, getting that product to market and reaching those early milestones for success in a company—great! This is on everyone's wish list, of course, but there is also plenty of support for first-time founders who are open to building expertise to fill in any knowledge gaps.

It comes down to demonstrating your commitment, and particularly that you are all in and dedicated to this journey. A typical investor view would pose this to the founder: 'Would you bet your house on what you're working on?' If you're not all in, then how can a third-party investor be convinced to come in on the journey?

You must be a good 'storyteller' as, ultimately, those early days before your product is in the market you have to sell the dream and what you're building, so being a good storyteller about what you're building is important. I talk about tenacity and resilience in this book as a fundamental requirement to be an entrepreneur and as Kirsten says, a certain level of 'being able to get up and keep going' is really important as it's a hard journey and there are always a lot of knock-backs on the way.

How validated do the business models need to be?

For seed-stage companies, Artesian can invest pre-revenue—but every company is different, every sector is different, every business model is different and every fund is different. The seed stage is all about the team and the vision.

Series A is about market traction, but traction may not necessarily mean revenue. A software company may be measured by revenue, whereas a space company may be measured by partnerships, field trials and manufacturing strategies that set you up for commercialisation, but it doesn't necessarily have to be revenue in that case. The later the stage the company is in, the more it is linked to traditional financial metrics.

The definitions of 'seed' and 'Series A' are slightly different between the United States and Australia. Australia's definition of a seed-stage company still has some expectations of leaning slightly more towards later stage, and where Australia is starting to get better, a true seed deal is an early-stage company. It's okay if they don't have a product in the market; it's okay if they don't have revenue.

(continued)

Market traction that could represent product market fit when you're too early to be selling your product could be validated by answering these questions:

- Have you been through an accelerator program (which teaches the basics of business growth)?

- Have you attracted some early capital from strategic angels who really understand your industry sector?

- What depth of interviews and market validation of the problem you're solving has been undertaken?

Amount to raise and 'use of funds'

Kirsten says, 'Start-ups are very fluid so often the use of funds they put to us is not how it plays out'.

The point I raise in this book is that it's more about the exercise itself and demonstrating the discipline involved. You should have a view of what your company is going to look like over the next three years, and if you've raised X amount of money, how would you use it to get there and add value.

Kirsten agrees and adds that it clarifies what the development milestones are that they need to achieve, which also speaks to where they will be at their next raise. This helps to backfill where they are now, and where they're going to be by the time they need to go back out to the market to raise more capital. Will that be enough to increase their valuation and will they be able to raise money at that next decision point to keep the company going?

These are always on the investor's list of questions:

- What is the use of funds?

- How long will it last you?

- Where will the company be by the next raise?

Exit strategy

The potential to exit is of significant importance to VC funds and investors in general. The VC will do a lot of thinking around investment proposals to validate the strategy. They often see presentations whose exit strategy is to exit via an IPO (initial public offering or public float), or by selling to someone in particular, and while that's good the VC will spend time focusing on the value of the strategy. The VC looks at every decision from a fund returns perspective. They will consider, among other things, how long it will be in their portfolio for their money in today and what they think they can sell it for at the end.

South Australian Venture Capital Fund (SAVCF): an example of a VC managing a government fund

The SAVCF was originally set up as a Series A and B co-investment fund only, but with Artesian's input it has been re-structured to enable smaller seed stage investing. The fund can now make seed investments up to a maximum of $400,000 and can also lead these deals with its own term sheet and without a co-investor. However, the more investors, the merrier, which of course provides more confidence in the round and more likelihood of it progressing.

Investments under this new mandate are now underway and in South Australia this is where the capital is needed most—not in the Series A or B rounds but in the pre-seed and seed stages. This brings South Australia in line with the rest of the country, where Artesian has funds capable of these types of early-stage investments.

Kirsten's advice to founders

For companies that are getting ready to fundraise or thinking about fundraising, Kirsten says, 'Don't be shy about reaching out and having a conversation' as that's part of an investor's job. Having the conversation, even if they aren't ready, can add some value to help them get ready and guide their business model development so it becomes a good fit for investment in the future.

(continued)

Artesian can also help startups understand whether they should be talking to them or to a different fund about their business, depending on the sector expertise required. Kirsten is very encouraging about companies coming to talk to them about their journey and reinforces that most venture capital funds generally have an 'open door' policy and are happy to take a meeting to see if they can be helpful. VC funds are always looking for deal flow, so the earlier they can see and guide companies, the better for everyone.

Kirsten would also encourage founders to understand the VC model, and what a VC backable business really looks like. 'We back great founders with a highly scalable business model, which is the foundation of what is an investible company to us.' Founders must be able to sell a big vision and big market opportunity, compared to a small business mindset which is still quite common in the Australian business community.

Finally, try not to get hung up on valuation. It can be a very frustrating topic, particularly for early-stage companies. Your pre-money valuation is a function of:

- how much capital you need
- how much of your company you want to hold at the end of the day
- what someone is willing to pay for it, and whether it makes sense
- how much money you need to raise to get to your next round.

Essentially ...

- How will you raise funds to start your venture? Will you fund it yourself or with other founders, family or close friends, or through an angel investor? Are there grants available (but keep in mind that grants will require private money to partly match the grant)?

- If you're looking for an angel investor, do you just want a financial investor, or do you want someone who can contribute skills and networks as well as money?

- Prepare an investor presentation and follow the slide deck topics in this chapter and the example slide deck on the companion website: www.essentialentrepreneur.com

- Position your company in the media and talk publicly about any successes or awards to get the attention of potential investors.

CHAPTER 12

Ownership and equity

This chapter addresses some more complex topics, but they're very important for when you bring on partners or investors in the business, so stay with me here.

What's the long-term vision of your business, and do you have all the skills necessary to complete that journey? Are you planning for your company to be self-funding, or will you need external finance to support the journey? Will that come from the bank or from external investors, or both, and do you want those potential investors to be actively involved in the running of the business?

These are the fundamental questions you'll need to ask yourself when contemplating partners and investment in your business. It's super important to hold as much equity as you can, but not to be foolish enough to limit your business and put it at risk of failing by not having the skills or the appropriate level of finance on board to navigate the journey ahead and achieve your goals.

There's always a fine balance when it comes time to raise money early in your business's life, as during the early validation period, while you're still testing potential products and services on customers, your business will be seen as a very risky venture for investors. The more risk involved, the more of your company they will want to own for less money, so only ever raise as much money as you need to get you through to the next milestone in your business plan. Demonstrate to your investors that you have successfully been able to achieve what you said you would and that you have added value to their investment.

When I ask start-ups how much they want to raise I often hear a huge figure, generally in the millions, so we then have a conversation around how much they really need to get to the next stage and I explain why. Generally, it's much, much less… and always results in a much better outcome and a faster raise.

The further you can 'de-risk' your business by demonstrating real revenue and profits, and a growing customer base, the more your business will suddenly have a real value and the more likely that investors will be willing to pay more money for a smaller shareholding. Giving away too much shareholding in the early stages of your business for relatively small amounts of money makes it difficult to raise significant money later without substantially diluting both the founders' and earlier investors' positions. Having numerous small shareholders can also become time consuming and distracting because you have to keep everyone happy—one or two larger shareholders is more manageable.

Assigning shareholdings

Coming from a family with a strong food and logistics background meant my brothers and I had the skills required to see the journey through with Regency Food Services. However, navigating the complex rules and regulations of the electricity market as ZEN Energy transformed from a solar and battery company to a large-scale electricity retailer was certainly beyond my existing skillset at the time.

This became a task of bringing key industry people together who provided different pieces of the jigsaw puzzle, from grid-scale battery technology to industry and government influence, to large-scale demand for energy. It's far better to own a smaller share of a large, successful business than a big share of nothing, which is often an entrepreneur's greatest mistake.

If you decide you need partners who can bring with them certain industry experience or technology, as well as investment for you to undertake the journey, then there are several ways you can structure such an agreement.

In the early stages of setting up a business, where different partners might be contributing a different combination of time, skills and cash, entrepreneurs may choose a flexible model of shareholding as some may provide more cash and less time, while others may provide more time and expertise but less cash. Their shareholding needs to be tied to these contributions so that if they put in less time or cash than initially promised they know there will be adjustments at certain points.

The issue in Australia is that this method can trigger both corporate law and tax implications each time a shareholding formally changes and complicates arrangements, unless a super complicated and expensive model is in place requiring extensive tax advice to set up. Most lawyers in Australia avoid this approach; it's nice in theory but complicated in reality. It's a popular model in the United States but doesn't work well within our corporate and tax context in Australia, which is set up to work with defined interests.

The flexible model may work between founders under a 'handshake agreement' in the early stages, but when things settle down and it comes time to formally assign shareholdings, this is usually done by issuing a fixed number of shares to each shareholder at a particular moment in time. Lawyers tend to work with actual numbers of shares issued—for example, '20000 ordinary shares' rather than '20 per cent of the company'. Founders typically create their own internal 'cap table' (a capital table listing investors and their shareholding—usually just a spreadsheet) that shows the percentage split, while 'official' legal documents such as shareholder agreements, a member register and ASIC records show the number of shares.

In Australia, we would usually rely on a separate shareholder agreement for a company to set out—among its shareholders, including founders and investors—provisions about how that relationship will work, including dealing with things such as control. If you as the founder own a shareholding of over 50 per cent of the issued share capital, you own a large enough share to control the company. Having control of the company enables you to control the makeup of the board of directors as well as the powers necessary to run the day-to-day operations, which also ensures your interests are protected. This may not sit so well with incoming minority shareholders, and they may want their say in certain decisions and not to be left to the mercy of those who own over 50 per cent of the shareholding. (The method for doing this is generally via a shareholder agreement, which I will talk about shortly.)

Such matters are usually noted as critical business matters and would typically be listed in the agreement under management and decision making. If, for example, the salary reviews of the CEO or founder(s) working in the business wasn't listed as a critical business matter requiring minority investors to agree to, then the working founders could decide through a majority to pay themselves double the day after receiving investment in the business. This wouldn't make for very happy investors and could cause immediate problems in the relationship. Investors want to see their money put into the business plan and how those funds will be used.

Shareholder agreements

There are some key issues for founding shareholders and new share-holders or investors coming into the business to consider when forming a shareholder agreement. We'll explore those now.

Shareholdings don't have to be equal

A common trap that people often fall into when starting a business is to go 50/50, which is nice and non-confrontational in the beginning. But business is all about making critical and timely decisions, and when you're not on the same page later on you'll find out the hard way that 50/50 isn't shared control, it's in fact no control! It can be debilitating and dysfunctional for a business if it can't make an important decision quickly and decisively, and it can eventually become a market disadvantage leading to potential failure. Where there are two equal shareholders, each has the right to 'veto', or not pass, a proposal since there's no majority party.

Giving minority shareholders a say in critical business matters

You can include a defined list of critical business matters in the shareholder agreement to give minority shareholders a voice. This is a list of items in the shareholder's agreement that require a defined special majority of votes, including those of minority investors. The default company constitution usually stipulates that 50 per cent of directors' votes is required for decision making. However, minority investors may want the right to veto critical decisions about the payment of dividends, selling the company, changing the nature of the company, key employment contracts, loans and guarantees, or contracts over a certain value or duration. Special voting rights in favour of the minority investors are therefore set out in the critical business matters list so that those decisions can't be made without the vote of the minority investors and shareholders.

Preference shares

Look out for preference shares in an investment proposal or term sheet. A term sheet outlines the (commonly) non-binding commercial terms by which an investor will make a financial investment in your company and is applicable to all equity investments, whether they be a smaller angel investor or a large venture capital fund. These terms are reflected in the shareholder or subscription agreements once agreed on.

The most common form of preference is where the preference share-holder is able to have funds returned to them ahead of others in certain situations. If everything goes well and the business is a success, preference shares don't cause an issue. However, in the case of a wind-up if the business fails, the investor holds a preference to get their money out first. For example, if the investor puts in $1 million, and the company fails and the assets are sold for $800 000, the investor takes it all and you as the founder get nothing.

These days, a preference position of 1× the investment is usually the default position. Generally, you won't see a request for preference shares from private angel investors on a low investment base but it's more prevalent for higher investments, particularly from VC funds investing larger sums for early-stage capital raises.

There are participating or non-participating preferences. 'Participating' means after the investor receives their preference payment (effectively getting their investment out) they then still participate on the balance of the funds raised in the shareholder ratio returning a profit on their investment. A 'non-participating' 1× preference means the investor gets their money out but does not participate in the balance of funds, which are then split among the other shareholders. Most preference shares are non-participating, but the terms would allow the investor to elect to 'convert' the preference shares into ordinary shares. In practice, investors don't usually convert to ordinary shares unless this leaves them better off—for example, where there's an exit through a sale transaction, or an IPO or where they end up with more return with ordinary shares.

There are also many different variations of preference shares, and the *Australian Corporations Act* allows for these different preference share terms if they are in the constitution, or if they are agreed on by shareholders.

Anti-dilution clauses

New businesses that are growing rapidly may need to raise several rounds of financing from investors, which is all good if the business plan, including the use of investors' funds, is working, the company keeps increasing in value and all investments made in the company therefore continue to increase in value.

A problem arises though when the company goes to raise further funds but can only raise those funds at a lower share price than the previous round, resetting the company's valuation and therefore devaluing the shareholdings of earlier investors. Who takes the valuation loss? Should all parties including the founders take a shared proportionate loss in value (which won't sit well with the earlier investors) or should the founder take all the loss and the first investor retain their value and/or percentage holding of the company in full? Or should the founder and the first investor share the loss but in an agreed ratio that favours the first investor?

In Australia it's not uncommon that early investors will insist on an anti-dilution clause of some sort to be effected in the case of a 'down round' where a lower share price is offered than the previous investment round. The worst position for a founder is to agree to a full ratchet anti-dilution clause, whereby the founder is forced to take the full loss of a devaluation, which can significantly impact the founder's shareholding percentage. This can also have the impact of disincentivising the founder if they are suddenly a minority shareholder in their own business and cause further problems for all investors. On the other hand, if there was no anti-dilution clause, all earlier investors, and the founder, proportionally reduce their share valuations. The investors may feel uneasy about this when they aren't actively involved in the running of the company and may believe the founder should take more of the impact for the loss in value. To avoid this, a middle ground scenario has been developed called the 'weighted average cost method'. It uses an agreed formula, which is skewed towards the founder, to share the loss, but the investors also share some of the pain. It basically reflects an average price between two different capital raising prices based on the number of shares in each round, but then adjusted (weighted) through a series of 'goal-seeking' mathematical calculations so the correct second-round shareholding is achieved.

These calculations and the formulas involved can be quite complex, so to accompany this book I have developed a companion website (www .essentialentrepreneur.com) that has a model for calculating both pre- and post-investment impacts on shareholdings, valuations and who takes how much of the loss, as well as other extended material and examples that can be continually updated based on requests. I can't emphasise enough the importance of understanding the impact of anti-dilution clauses on your business. This doesn't mean you can necessarily avoid them, but at least you're coming into the agreement with your eyes wide open and can negotiate the best outcome through a weighted average approach if possible, not forgetting this only has an impact if the valuation of the company decreases.

Drag-along, tag-along rights

Minority investors who invest later in the journey don't necessarily want to be 'dragged' into a deal to sell the company unless they have achieved their targeted return, whereas founders always want to drag minority investors in if a deal is on the table that suits them and the purchaser wants to buy the entire company. So, an acceptable outcome needs to be negotiated.

Tag-along provisions, on the other hand, aim to protect the minority shareholders from being stranded when the majority shareholder sells. When a tag-along provision is in place it ensures that the same terms and conditions of the sale are extended to the minority shareholders, allowing them to tag along in the deal and sell their shares along with the majority at the same price, terms and conditions.

Good leaver vs bad leaver

These are generally a set of conditions enacted when a key founder leaves the company. A founder or key person leaving and taking fundamental knowledge and IP on the operation of the business can cause enormous upheaval and potentially lead to a business failure.

Sometimes the exit can't be avoided due to matters such as health issues or family breakdowns. In this case, where it's out of the person's control, it is generally accepted that that person would be deemed a 'good leaver' and any shares or options that they are forced to relinquish under their arrangements with the company generally would be bought back/paid out at or around market value. This is different from a situation where a key person leaves who is in control of their personal situation and deemed to be manipulating or purposefully jeopardising the business outcome. This is deemed a 'bad leaver' and it is generally accepted that bad leavers should not get full value of their shares or options that they are forced to hand back, and therefore the value of such shares or options in the company is significantly reduced.

Reporting clauses

Investors will want a reasonable reporting regime on their investment to feel reassured that the business is on track. However, you as the founder do not want this to be so onerous that it becomes a distraction and time consumer, so it's good to agree on a reporting regime at the outset that is manageable.

Agree on how much reporting is required and what the frequency of reporting should be. If you have a number of investors and some are large and significant compared to others, the larger investors may require, or be offered, substantially more reporting. This could be managed through their subscription agreement rather than the shareholder agreement, so that it is unique to the shareholder.

Options and warrants

Some potential investors will take up options in the company if they are contributing to the company's operations either on the board or through providing other skills and services that the company can't afford to pay market rates for. This is an option provided by the company to the potential investor to invest at a pre-determined point in the future and at a pre-determined price instead of putting cash in now, which is a much less riskier position for an early-stage company. It allows a potential investor to trade their skills now for options on a shareholding at an agreed time in the future at an agreed price now (strike price), which could be a heavily discounted price if the company significantly increases its value between now and then.

Options have key elements, such as exercise price (agreed price that will be paid), exercise period (possibly two or three years into the future) and vesting (conditions that must be satisfied before those options can be exercised). These are crucial in determining how well options work as an incentivisation tool to complement what you're trying to achieve.

We also see options being used as part of an incentive package for employees of start-ups or early-stage companies where the company can't pay the regular market salary. Depending on how these options are structured, there will be varying tax consequences, and if done correctly these are a good incentive. If done poorly, they will penalise the employee from a tax perspective, which is not ideal.

Warrants are similar to options and are issued directly by a company to an investor, but the term is usually used with listed companies and not so relevant to the start-up space.

The Australian Investment Council (www.avcal.com.au) is a good place to start when looking for templates of shareholder and other seed investment agreements. These template agreements, although originally designed to favour the investor, have over the years been seen as the starting point for many investment deals—and commonly used as standard documents for many angel investors, VC funds and companies. The balance to be negotiated with an investor is primarily reflected in the points above and should be discussed with a solicitor with early-stage investment experience. You can also find other open-sourced legal documents for capital raising through other incubators or VC groups—but care should be taken to make sure they are appropriate (i.e. Australian based—or your home region—vs US/Silicon Valley based).

Bringing on investors and partners into your business can be a fundamental key to success, but also a fast track to failure if you lock yourself in with the wrong people who don't turn out like you thought they would. It's very hard to then break free of those relationships without a significant cost attached.

Try working with potential investors for a while before they actually invest so you get to know each other, and the investors have a chance to put their goodwill and passion for the business on display. Any increase in the potential valuation they contribute at this time should be taken into account when negotiating an investment or option position. You could form an advisory board in the first instance and see if they are willing to participate in that way for a trial period to see if the relationship works.

SWEAT's equity

The first version of the SWEAT business cost about $25 000, spent mainly on the eBooks and associated photography to get the business going, which Tobi and Kayla bootstrapped with the earnings from their personal training work. The margins made on the eBooks was very high, as once they were created it was virtually all profit from there on, so when combined with strong sales, they produced a solid positive cash flow that enabled them to continue funding the further reinvestment into what the company needed to go to the next stage.

For about two years, approximately 75 to 90 per cent of the free cash flow was reinvested into the business. Tobi states that

The business rigour early on was not very savvy, and investment was made very much on an "as needs" basis to serve a need that was right in front of us. There was very little strategic planning at that point.

Fleet Space's funding journey

The first year of Fleet was just Flavia and Matt building 'stuff' with their own money (bootstrapping), building small satellites in the garage. Matt invested $25 000 to buy parts so they were able to launch a satellite for proof of concept.

Based on this they were then able to raise a first (seed) round of $5 million. They were on a roll:

- After two years they had raised their Series A round of $7 million.

- A further two years later they had raised their Series B of $40 million.

- Now they are in the process of raising their Series C round and raising more consistently. What they have tried to do is triple their valuation with each raise.

For Haigh's it's all been self-funded

I asked Simon about whether the sense of responsibility for a multi-generational 107-year-old brand weighed heavily on their risk taking when making timely decisions on expansion:

> We've never been huge risk takers. We are not going out to finance our growth and take on equity to be the biggest company in our market. It's all been self-funded. Growth can be a double-edged sword for us because if you continue to grow retail you must also grow the manufacturing capacity that then needs to keep up. You can't just open another six stores without also funding the expansion of manufacturing to meet the added demand.

Further expansion of the factory is the next project and was well underway in 2022 with land secured in Salisbury (north of Adelaide) in preparation for the next step. Simon says this will be the home of online distribution and future production expansion.

Essentially ...

- Do you have all the skills for the journey, or do you need other skills in the business to achieve your goals?

- How much investment do you need to get you to the next milestone in your business plan? Don't raise more than you need to execute on your plan, otherwise it can become harder to add value to the investment.

- Do you need smart investors who come with skills and actively participate in directing the business, or do you only need the cash (known as dumb money)?

- Aim to de-risk your business as much as possible by demonstrating real revenue and profits as well as a growing customer base so investors can attribute a higher valuation, and you're not giving away too much shareholding in a small early raise.

- A well-drafted and well-thought-out shareholder agreement will clearly set out the rights and responsibilities of all shareholders and outline rules to resolve potential disputes, facilitate investment and define an exit process.

CHAPTER 13

Trademarks and patents

The valuation of a company can be substantially enhanced if the intellectual property (IP) of the company is protected. These are the things that create your sustainable advantage in the market—such as business names, logos, technical designs, processes, recipes and anything that can create a barrier for other companies to easily compete with you. This is usually done through trademarks and patents.

Trademarks (TM): protecting your brand

Deciding on the perfect brand, ensuring it's free to use and then protecting it are three of the most important steps you will take when starting a business. A good brand is the cut-through tool that's going to get the attention of your market and position your business within that market. Through your marketing and sales programs, you will be constantly investing in your brand and building value, which, when successful, others will quickly try to leverage from, so make sure you choose wisely and then protect it. When you look for investors on your business journey, protection of your brand is one of the first things they will ask you about.

You need to ensure the brand you want is available for the business name (entity), the internet domain (www), Instagram, Facebook and any other media platforms you may want to use either now or in the future. Checking the availability of your brand in your country will not be enough if you have international ambitions, so searches of trademark registers in other countries, common law searching and Google type searching must be part of your approach. To best achieve that aim, the brand needs to be unique and memorable and may also be accompanied by a tagline to further describe what you do and/or the business's aspirations.

Strong brands also have a smart connection to what your product or service is. ZEN, for me, was an acronym for Zero ENergy (balancing energy generation and demand) but also connected strongly to Eastern philosophies around enlightenment, exploring a new way of living and embracing wisdom. The brand 'ZEN' followed by the market I had defined gave me the initial business name I wanted—ZEN Home Energy Systems—which was later curtailed to ZEN Energy as we transitioned to a full-service energy company incorporating electricity retailing. Note the difference between the brand 'ZEN' and the descriptive elements 'home energy systems' and 'energy'.

Once you decide on a brand and have done some broad searching across the internet to determine it is not being used, or closely resembles something already being used in the market you want to be in, then quickly reserve it on all platforms. Also check all regions overseas that you want to potentially trade in so you don't end up in a position where you can't expand to other markets under that brand if successful.

Applying for trademark registration

In common law countries (including Australia), once you start trading and building your reputation in the market, you automatically receive brand protection, but only in the local geographic region where you are trading. This could be defined as those areas that you are advertising and selling in but does *not* include all of Australia. It's vital that you keep records of proof of use of the brand for reputational protection, which can include copies of advertisements, brochures, any media use and sales invoices that carry your brand name. It's also strongly recommended to immediately use the 'TM' symbol on or in connection with the brand when you go to market to warn the market that it is intended to be your brand. To your benefit you will also, from a trademark registration perspective, claim 'first user rights' in the respective country.

To enable extended protection across the whole of the country you will need to file an application for trademark registration in your country. Doing this will also provide a 'priority date', not only in your country so that your mark has priority over subsequent use or applications for the same mark for the same or related goods and services after the filing date, but also in other countries where a trademark system exists as part of a shared international protocol. The protocol recognises that trademark applicants in those countries signatory to the protocol also have six months within which to file into your country and claim their earlier filing date as the effective filing date in your country. The protocol deems that they can claim priority for their mark over yours. Therefore, it is important to note that this system means it can be at least seven months before you can be sure that your mark is clear for registration in your country.

Designing your brand, logo and tagline

Alongside the brand there's generally a logo, and sometimes a tagline, that assists to position your business in the market. It is important from the start to put effort into the whole design that encapsulates your brand, logo and tagline, as this can present your business as having credibility and demonstrates professionalism from the start. A hastily put together design, on the other hand, can portray an amateur, cheap and not-so-credible or professional business and may lose you potential customers before you start. I always recommend engaging a professional graphic designer from early on to produce an engaging and professional style guide to represent your brand that works well and consistently across all media and platforms. It's the best way to get your business off to a flying start and gives you a strong document to start discussions with a trademark attorney about your proposed trademark and strategy. The individual elements in your design can be trademarked (protected) separately or combined as the design or 'mark' that identifies your business.

When you do engage a professional designer or web developer it's very important to ensure you own the copyright of the logo. Often developers or designers will own the copyright by default (or it's in the contract, so read every contract carefully and understand what it means) and you end up not being the owner of the copyright of your own brand. This can prove very problematic and costly as you move forward and grow the business. You will want to broaden the use of the brand and all its elements, so make sure you negotiate to have full ownership of the brand, logo, tagline and designs early, as you want to have copyright for all future uses.

If you are relying on first use rights as protection, it is also important to understand that your brand and logo can't evolve or change over your start-up journey. A changed logo can be considered a significantly different logo for this purpose, and you may lose protection of the earlier brand even though the two versions may seem similar to you.

Consulting a trademark attorney

Regarding strategy and dealing with the mechanics of trademark filing, I always recommend talking to a trademark attorney early, as it's a complicated area in regard to ownership of the brand, protection rights and what you actively need to pursue protection for, and in what countries, as this should be dictated by your plans to expand. An attorney who specialises in trademarks will help you handle this important asset of your business and advise on many issues, including what can and can't be protected, as well as managing the process, since you will be quickly juggling the many other things that you need to take care of in a rapidly growing early-stage business. I have personally found it is worth the investment to have a professional dealing with the mechanics and to ensure the process is done correctly the first time.

There are 45 different classes of which most relate to goods and some to services, and your product or service may cross over more than one of these categories so a listing in more than one may be required. Trademark attorneys have the skill to decide which classes apply and what words to use to provide the coverage you require now and into the future. They will have a long-term view in mind and will generally encourage you to file with a broad selection of goods and services that represent not only the goods and services you are offering now, but also those you have an intention to offer in the future. A trademark attorney will often provide early guidance for no fee, but must, before they are engaged, provide a quotation for the work they will do for you. Some are great and provide guidance upfront to get you on the right track and once you create a trusted relationship with them, they can join you on the journey of creating a brand strategy that will support your business for the present and into the future.

A ballpark cost to engage a professional trademark attorney and apply for one brand in one class is generally under AUD$1000. This cost includes many considerations that an attorney is trained to consider, including discussing ownership of the brand, the suitability of the proposed trademark for acceptance, determining the appropriate goods and services for which the brand will be used presently and over the next three years. The attorney will remind you about the need to use your mark on all the goods and services for which the mark is registered, since you cannot reserve the mark forever. However, a single use is sufficient to preserve the registration since you don't want the mark to be challenged after the initial three years for non-use. Your trademark attorney will also check all the details of the application, ensure the dates of each step and action involved in the process are consistent with the legal requirements, and most importantly check the registration certificate to ensure accuracy before providing it to you. These checks and attention to detail are absolutely worth the costs if you are serious about protecting your trademark.

In Australia there is a fast way to check whether a trademark is likely or not to be accepted by the trademarks office. That system is referred to as the HeadStart process. It's an adjunct to the standard trademark application system. HeadStart applications are not advertised, so no-one knows you've tried to register a particular mark and it's not exposed publicly at that point. The trademarks office will pick up the application under this process within days of application and will perform a preliminary examination. It will then provide a report to the applicant or their attorney. The preliminary report will only outline whether the trademark is clear or will identify broadly stated issues that may block acceptance of the trademark. An attorney can help to provide an assessment of the seriousness of the issues raised. Some issues may be resolved by argument or the use of evidence of prior use; some issues may be too hard to overcome and, if so, the HeadStart process allows the applicant the option to halt the trademark application process.

Consulting a trademark attorney, even if you've made your own application, is again a smart move, as it allows you to discuss more broadly the ownership, breadth of the mark and likelihood of obtaining acceptance. A good attorney will have the experience to know which objections can be successfully challenged and which won't.

The cost of using a trademark attorney to apply for a trademark using the HeadStart process in Australia is roughly AUD$900 (stage 1 is about $600 and stage 2 is about $300. You may get back $300 if you choose not to proceed with stage 2). There will be the attorney's costs for providing advice between the issue of the preliminary report and the payment, or not, of the second part fee depending on the number of issues raised and remedies available to challenge any potential obstacles. There will be further costs in getting the trademark accepted and finally registered, but your attorney will always provide those costs upfront and have your best interests in mind.

In summary, a good trademark attorney will provide a strong initial and ongoing filing strategy and help you navigate a logical and experienced pathway through the trademark use and registration process. Often ignored is the cost of getting things wrong: not only the monetary cost, but also the immeasurable cost of your time devoted to avoiding or dealing with roadblocks later in the life of your brand. Good advice and guidance at the right time can ensure your brand will come to represent the goodwill of your business, so choose and treat your brand accordingly.

Registered design rights

As we have seen, trademarks are generally used to distinguish your goods and services from those of your competitors and can include words, logos, sounds, shapes and colours. A registered design, however, can go further towards protecting the overall aesthetics and visual appearance of your product, including the shape, colour and ornamentation. A trademark attorney will help advise on your overall strategy, including the need for a registered design.

In Australia, having a registered design, combined with an enforceable protection over it, is a two-part process:

- *Step 1* is to register the design; however, this does not give you the right to enforce it. The maximum time you can register a design for is 10 years broken into two, five-year periods. The cost is AUD$250 per design for the first five years plus $450 to renew it for the second five-year period, in addition to a similar cost for an attorney's support.

- *Step 2* is the certification (examination) of the registered design, which, if it passes and is subsequently certified, you have the legal right to enforce. The cost to request an examination is $420 or a competitor can request the examination of your design if it concerns them, which you will have to pay half of. Additional fees will apply for extensions and certificate copies.

The main point to remember here is that a trademark can effectively last forever if used and renewed, but Australian registered design rights have a maximum life of 10 years.

Patents: novel innovations

Patents are a complicated area, so bear with me here. It's good information to know even if you're not considering a patent.

Patents relate to a particular technical innovation that can be a product or the technology or process behind the product or service that you provide. Patents, however, are only one form of intellectual property (IP). Trade secrets, copyright, trademarks and even a price guide and client lists can be just as important (or even more important in certain circumstances). By properly identifying and protecting your IP (your market advantage) you are creating and building value within your business for yourself and other shareholders.

Again, I would strongly recommend talking to an experienced patent attorney early in the process as they can give much better insight than a patent search analysis alone can. They will ask questions about the differentiating factors: Has it been done before in the same or a similar way? What business model are you using and how does your idea assist in supporting your business? Your job is to help them understand the differentiating factors and lay the groundwork for determining whether it is potentially novel and patentable. The attorney will need to determine the following:

- Is it patentable subject matter?

- Is it new/novel compared to everything that has been published anywhere in the world?

- Does it have an inventive step (not obvious to those who are skilled in the art of the invention)?

The patenting process can be complex and lengthy, and there are many steps involved in obtaining a granted patent. There are some parts of the process you can do yourself, with guidance from an attorney, to reduce your costs.

Step 1: Searching

A search can be done informally by you or an attorney, who may engage a searching company (general cost range is AUD$500 to $1500 for a novelty search). You may not be interested in obtaining a patent yourself, but you should be very interested in whether you infringe the patent rights of others, so an attorney can organise and advise on your freedom to operate. You don't want to spend a lot of money setting up a business only to get stopped in your tracks by a patent infringement once you start trading!

Google Patents (patents.google.com) is a great place to start searching for existing or similar patents. Searching is done on the full text, not just titles and abstracts, but you need to know how to search, which is where consulting a patent attorney is useful. For example, attorneys are trained to assist you with understanding the terminology used by different cultures for describing their invention and for translating details of your invention to others.

Another useful search engine for patents is Espacenet (worldwide. espacenet.com), which is run by the European Patent Office (EPO). Most member states of the EPO have an Espacenet service in their national language, and access to the EPO's worldwide database, most of which is in English and contains data on more than 130 million patent documents.

As there are so many patent documents globally, another way of searching is via a landscape search, which uses algorithms to identify groups of patents related to the field you're searching. This provides a virtual topographic map to group patents into classes and fields of relevance and, most importantly, identifies gaps that can be focused on for greater success in obtaining rights for novel ideas.

Landscape searching comes at a much higher cost (tens of thousands) due to the technical detail covered and the benefit it provides. It also provides companies investing in research and development with tremendous insight on where to focus their efforts and expense when developing new technologies.

Step 2: Analysing search results

You can draw your own conclusions, which may well be evident from your own search, particularly if there are already a lot of patents in the area you're looking at. If you're uncertain how to interpret the results or are overwhelmed by the process, I would advise you to consult a patent attorney to determine whether an opportunity exists for your product or technology/process in the market you are targeting.

Having the search done professionally helps the patent attorney formulate an opinion, which can have considerable value. Advantageously, if there's a need or want to draft a patent application, then the attorney is in a position to draft a much stronger patent, rather than just relying on the inventor's knowledge of the 'prior art' (a term used by patent attorneys when referring to existing patents).

When lodging a patent, you must be very clear about who is the inventor (or inventors). This area of patent law is filled with misunderstanding and missteps that have brought undone well-intentioned applicants. It's best to ensure this issue is considered early to avoid unwanted and potentially damaging claims down the track, especially if investors are involved, since they want certainty that this issue is done and dusted. Big problems can emerge if co-inventors aren't listed on an application, or an inventor is listed who isn't actually an inventor, as these circumstances can potentially make a patent invalid.

Step 3: Lodging a provisional patent (priority date)

A provisional patent, once lodged, gives you a priority date for 12 months (a 'first to file' date of invention) but a provisional is only a patent application with a limited life of 12 months, so a decision needs to made on the commercial importance of that invention and whether you proceed to the completion stage within that 12-month period. A trap that people often fall into is bundling too many ideas into one provisional patent specification, when not all the ideas may make it to the subsequent complete patent application. Those inventions not covered will be exposed when a single patent (the final chosen idea) becomes a published document six months into the next completion stage of the patent process. A copy of the original provisional patent specification can be requested from that point and would expose all the other ideas, which may still have potential. These can no longer be protected as the priority date has lapsed and those ideas are then available to the public and competitors for free use.

The official fee to lodge a provisional patent is very small, but the value ultimately lies in the likely essence and scope of the invention described in the patent specification. To ensure that the provisional patent specification is properly written and includes sufficient detail for the best chance of success, I would advise you to consult a patent attorney. Depending on the amount of work involved, you could expect to pay between $4000 and $8000 in Australia for developing a professionally written provisional patent and having it lodged.

Step 4: Completing the patent

This stage needs to be commenced within the 12-month window of the provisional patent, which begins on the filing date (priority date), as the provisional patent will lapse on the anniversary of that date. You can choose to further enhance the filed provisional patent by filing another provisional patent specification each time there's a significant improvement or modification to the preceding provisional. Sometimes the 12 months passes too quickly. It's possible during that time to re-file the same or a modified provisional patent specification, but doing that will create a new filing and hence a new priority date will be set. You then take the risk that another similar patent has been lodged in that period that you've let go.

The most cost-effective way to complete a patent that provides the opportunity to file in many countries is to file a Patent Cooperation Treaty (PCT) application. This is a type of patent that allows you to file directly into the regional patent-receiving offices of the 152 countries that make up the PCT, which was formed in 1970.

A PCT application enables you to complete your patent application at a later time, beyond the often too-short 12-month period of the provisional patent application. The process includes a preliminary examination by one of the regional offices, which is a very valuable part of the overall process since it allows the patent applicant to gauge the likely view of a patent examiner as to the acceptance or rejection of their invention at an early stage of the patent process.

You can also submit a patent application independently to a targeted country that may not be a member of the PCT countries. It could simply be more economic and faster if you go through that targeted country's office rather than the PCT process since your business is only interested in protecting the invention in that specific country, or countries, as that's where your primary market is, or where the product is most likely to be manufactured.

A PCT application is very useful if you're not sure which countries you want to apply into as the PCT system allows 18 months within which to make the decision to file in one or more of the PCT countries. The cost of a PCT application is roughly AUD$10000 to $12000, which includes the preliminary examination cost and the drafting of the patent specification, which is the most important document in the process.

The specification includes the body (the primary description), which must support the full breadth of the claimed invention and can't be amended in the future, together with the all-important claims, which define the invention. These specifications need to be precise, as the use of a term such as 'comprises' instead of 'includes' can make all the difference.

Step 5: Filing

PCT countries have different due dates of lodgement for what's referred to as the 'national phase' via the PCT system.

Filing of a PCT application into a local country's office is typically undertaken by your attorney's local agent in the respective country.

Filing must be completed within 30 months from the original priority date of the *provisional* patent (31 months in some countries), as this combines the 12 months from the provisional application and the additional 18 months for the international phase of the PCT application process. Occasionally, some countries may also require an assignment (transfer) from the inventor to the owner of the patent before filing.

Each 'national phase' application (individual country application) can cost between AUD$2000 and $4000 per country, and becomes more expensive when translation is required. The examination process (often referred to as the 'prosecution' phase) and granting processes of the patent for each country can literally take years, and maybe even longer after renewals have taken place (yes, in some countries, you'll pay for renewals for an application that hasn't been officially granted yet!). Renewal fees for the application may also vary from patent office to patent office, and can be huge in the European office, for instance, since it covers the potential to enter 23 countries in that region. Your attorney will assist with the strategy and will manage the dates and renewals as they become due and you can decide whether to continue or not, which is another reason why patent attorneys become essential in the process.

This drawn-out and costly process has a dual purpose: to support the funding of the local patents offices, and also to act as a disincentive to maintain a patent that's not a commercial success thereby helping to clean up the patent register.

As mentioned, in some countries the full specification will need to be translated into the official local language. If this is required, it can be a costly exercise, as the technical translation must be accurate. The cost of a local language translation can be in the vicinity of a further AUD$5000 to $10 000 so the whole application and prosecution process can be an expensive exercise. However, if the patent is a key part of the valuation of a business worth potentially millions or billions of dollars, then applying for and protecting its intellectual property, including brands, business model and technology, can easily be justified.

Fleet Space's patents serve their customers' needs

When they started Fleet Space, Flavia and Matt had the idea for the business but didn't have the technology. They built the technology as they went along based on what they were seeing in the field and what their customers wanted.

Six years later, they had 30 patents from building technology designed to service their actual customer needs, and not based on hypotheticals. Flavia says, 'This comes back to the validation model, building the technology and resulting patents around customer needs. These are now very valuable patents!'

Haigh's experience with patents

Simon explains that there's very little you can patent in the confectionery industry: 'Larger companies have trademarks on things like "freckles" and Cadbury has tried to trademark its unique shade of purple'.

Apart from some unique packaging designs, there's not a lot that can be protected because it's all common knowledge. The original Haigh's emblem and the name 'Haigh's' are trademarked. 'Trying to protect anything that has been copied overseas is near impossible', says Simon.

Essentially ...

- If you are successful in your business, there will be a flood of people trying to leverage off your business name, copy your business model or copy your technology, so protection through trademarks, registered designs and patents, where possible, is essential for long-term business valuation protection. Think of it as the same as protecting other confidential intellectual property.

- There is protection in common law countries if you can prove you are first to market, but only in the local region you're trading in.

- When granted, a patent will give you exclusive commercial rights to your invention. This allows you to stop others manufacturing, using or selling your invention/technology and enables you to license the manufacturing of your invention or use of your technology to others.

- Obtaining a patent is a long process, starting with a provisional patent that provides a 'priority date' for an initial 12 months while you decide on your longer term protection strategy.

- Don't put too many ideas into one provisional patent application as they will all be potentially exposed six months into the PCT process when the complete patent that relies on the provisional patent is published. The final document will usually focus on the one selected invention from those listed in the provisional, yet a request can be made for the original provisional, which will expose all the other ideas.

- Patent and trademark processes can have the benefit of protecting your business and the value you have created within the business, which is important for you, your family and your investors.

CHAPTER 14

What business am I in?

Many entrepreneurs fall into the trap of trying to be 'all things to all people'. They jump at every opportunity presented to them and in the process diminish their resources to the point where they don't do anything well, run out of cash and fail.

By nature, entrepreneurs see opportunities along the way that may be complementary, but not core, to their business. These 'opportunities' must be screened very carefully.

Staying focused

The temptation with a business, particularly after raising capital, is to try and do more. More is good if you're staying focused and true to your product and vision and adding value to your business, but if more means stretching yourself or your resources too thinly and doing things that don't add value to your core business, then you're losing focus and wasting valuable resources.

You might argue that you're developing an aligned market and that at some point in the future this will add value, but I implore you to always ask yourself, 'What business am I in, and would this add value to the business or put it at risk?'

Again, the key risk here is running out of money by not staying focused on the vision and mission of the business and trying to do too many things that aren't core to your success. As I say a few times in this book, but probably still not often enough: if you run out of money, it's game over!

A while back, one company came to me with a business model to build satellites. There are many people who want to build satellites, so the first thing I always ask is: what's going to make their satellites better than the next company's or what's their point of difference in the market? I like to drill down into where the value really lies in the business model. After some conversation and probing it became clear they had developed a very good altitude sensor and accompanying BUS (the communication system that transfers data between components inside the satellite). My next question was, 'Have you considered just having the best altitude sensor and satellite BUS on the market and selling that key component to all the satellite manufacturers?' (In other words, become like an Intel or AMD, which provides the processing chips for computer manufacturers.) This could more easily become their business model and require much less cash and outside expertise to get going.

Keeping it simple

Don't overcomplicate your business model. Instead, look for what it is you're doing that carries the real value and how you take that to market. If, down the track, there's an opening in the market to extend your product downstream and you have built cash reserves, or have the necessary financial backing, then you can always consider that option later on.

On the other hand, you could already be doing too much in your business unnecessarily and not even realising it. It's always good practice to review your business model and keep asking the questions, 'What business am I in?' and 'What are we really good at that makes us money?' — in other words, 'Where does the value in our business really lie?' — and then look to get rid of the things that don't make money.

When my brother Greg and I had our food distribution business, Regency Food Services, we asked ourselves these questions about halfway through the business's life and realised we were running three quite different businesses. We had a procurement business; a complex multi-temperature warehousing facility, including an advanced stock picking system; and a distribution fleet of very expensive multi-temperature zoned trucks driven by our own employed drivers.

We decided we were very good at the first two. The one causing us the most headaches was the delivery side of the business: owning and operating the truck fleet. Drivers would call in sick from time to time, throwing schedules into chaos; they would have accidents; trucks would break down; the refrigerator motors would break down; and the maximum orders we could deliver per truck appeared to be about 30 a day on average.

So we considered the idea of selling our trucks to our drivers, getting them into their own business and exclusively contracting them back. We worked with the drivers on a model that would generously reward them for performance based on a percentage of value delivered and would provide enough to cover the ongoing operating expenses, depreciation and maintenance on the trucks. The percentage was calculated based on their current average delivery value, so any increase in performance provided significant opportunity to earn more income. There were very strict clauses on representation and presentation as consistency in operation was particularly important to us.

Some were very keen; others were unsure and wanted to sit back and see how it worked for those who took up the option. We agreed a pilot would be a good way to proceed and arranged to contract our first two drivers. The result was instant and amazing. Those two trucks were suddenly able to achieve 50 deliveries or more a day each. The contracted owner drivers looked for every opportunity to deliver more and provide the best service they possibly could for 'their customers', which increased our sales. We no longer carried the headache of trucks breaking down and drivers being sick because they managed their own trucks and had contingency plans in place in case of unexpected incidents. This gave us the time and money to really progress and develop our core business, which was where our real skills and value lay. It represented our key point of difference and also produced the most profit.

ZEN Energy was another of our businesses that provided plenty of opportunity to do too much too quickly. As we were selling leading-edge technology to generate solar power for homes, I was constantly thinking how homes could use less energy to make the impact much greater. I was frustrated at how poorly houses were designed and built and how inefficient they were.

This led me to have numerous conversations with leading home builders about how they could build homes that would consume very little energy simply by focusing on aspect, ventilation, insulation, thermal mass and integrating technologies such as hydronic heating, solar hot water and solar PV (that is, photovoltaics: the process of converting sunlight into electrical energy) and energy storage (batteries).

The long-term cost of ownership of a home proved to be much less under this new model, coupled with having a home that was close to net zero emissions. The builders, however, saw the additional upfront cost as a barrier that would lose sales and were more focused on building a theatre room, with little concern about the environmental aspects and the operating cost and comfort of the home.

I found this lack of education in the market so frustrating that I seriously considered starting a new 'ZEN Homes' division of the business and introducing high-quality, sustainable homes to the market. It was against everything I had learned about staying focused and would have cost the company a fortune to get started (apart from not having the staff or skills to build complete homes). It would have potentially made a good partnership with an established builder who could leverage the ZEN brand, but builders just couldn't get past the enticement of simply building additional rooms and churning out more of the same poorly built mass-market homes.

It was around 2008 to 2010 that I adopted this mindset, but doing the right thing by the company at the time won out, and I stopped myself from going down that pathway. Today, though, it's interesting to see the demand from the public for more environmentally conscious and energy-efficient houses continually increasing as the market becomes more and more educated in how they can easily reduce the ongoing cost of home ownership by simply investing a bit more in the right design and building materials.

Focusing on SWEAT

I asked Tobi whether they outsourced their video production or did it in-house because it must have been tempting to build a production studio and own their equipment. Tobi says they went through phases of producing in-app content and creative brand campaigns, as well as the required social media production. For the fitness content they in-housed the 'thinking' — being the exercise science, project planning and management — and then would contract production crews and hire equipment as needed. It didn't make sense for them to own very expensive video production equipment (like a $300000 camera lens!) and camera technology was rapidly changing and continually improving.

They often debated building a full-blown production studio at their Adelaide offices. But then the pandemic hit. Tobi remembers thinking, 'What if we want to produce people from overseas and what if they can't travel?' They decided they had to have production studios overseas:

We decided not to own them but to effectively look for 'production as a service' and 'studio as a service' offerings around the world, which was incrementally more expensive from a per-video perspective

(continued)

but allowed for speed and freedom that we couldn't have achieved otherwise because we couldn't get people to Australia.

Tobi has the view that 'every business is a continually iterating hypothesis': you're effectively building your thesis on your business and over time all you're really doing is improving that with learning.

Focusing on what you do is one thing, but focusing on improving the theory of your business is another whole thing. What are the intricate and incremental financial levers that you're not understanding yet? An example being, 'we sell to women', but where, what age, how are their attitudes different, what are their preferences, how and when do they like to train? Over time you're adding more layers and understanding to your hypothesis and theory of your business.

Gradually, this enables a business to build its own capability as an organisation, which in turn creates its sustainable competitive advantage.

Flavia on her focus

Fleet Space is now focused almost exclusively on using satellites for mineral exploration, which is an application of its core mission of space communication and connectivity.

Haigh's and chocolate cafés

Simon says, 'There was a lot of pressure at one stage to open chocolate cafés. Lindt, Max Brenner and Guylian all opened cafés in Sydney – some have been successful and some not'. For Haigh's, a key part of the problem would have been the core trading periods of Easter and Christmas and how to manage the cafés over those times, as well as the dedicated space required for the café.

Essentially ...

- What is it that you do exceptionally well and what do you do that adds the most value to your business? Continue to do it well. Look for continual improvement in product and processes but stay focused on the core business without being distracted by non-core opportunities.

- Look to outsource the parts of your business that are non-core so you can again focus on what you do really well and where your intellectual property lies. This will add the most value to your business and generate the greatest opportunity to sell your business at a high price in the future.

- Be focused and be exceptional at what you do without spreading your resources too thin.

- Outsourcing non-core aspects of your business and selling off those assets can also free up cash to improve your core business.

CHAPTER 15

Tuning and restructuring

In business you need to be constantly watching the horizon as it's inevitable the market you're serving will change at some point, whether that's through government policy changes, technological changes, changes in trends or simply changes in people's needs. It's therefore super important to continually 'tune' your business to the market. If the market has undergone a fundamental change, you may need a significant restructure—and quickly—to preserve capital so that you live to play another day.

Market adaptability

There's an old saying: 'Hire slow and fire fast'. Take the time to find the right people to create the culture you're after in your business (this should be a higher priority than skills alone). With people who are passionate about the business and its mission you'll be in a much stronger position to weather any storm. These people will pitch in to cover more of the load in difficult times. And it goes both ways: make sure you support your team when times are good as well.

Nevertheless, if the market undergoes a fundamental change, you may need to cut staff fast. This is an incredibly difficult task for entrepreneurs, who will likely have become very close to their team members and will always fight to save their jobs—sometimes at the detriment of the entire business.

Demonstrating market adaptability to your bankers will give them confidence in you, and they, in turn, will be more likely to provide temporary financial flexibility if you are seen to be making necessary changes. Banks work on financial ratios and caveats and there's no disguising your performance when things go wrong, so it's much better to be on the front foot, make the call and demonstrate how you'll adapt to the situation.

Rapidly changing market conditions

Depending on the market you're in, market conditions can change rapidly and be totally out of your control. Many industries are subject to government policy of the time and subsequent interference when those policies change. A market may be incentivised at one point in time and those incentives may disappear just as quickly. General market changes—such as when the Reserve Bank decides to change interest rates, for example—may have an immediate impact on the property market.

Continually asking yourself 'What if?' is very good practice, and having a plan to meet unforeseen externalities will give your business an extra layer of resilience. In addition to the more predictable changes, we have also seen the full force of nature in recent years, including bushfires, floods, droughts and, most recently, a pandemic, so there are a lot of what ifs to consider! Mass cyber-attacks and geopolitical fallouts with traditional trading partners can also prompt us to pose the question of whether we have too many eggs in one basket or market. As our traditional market ages and their needs change, new competitors and new technology are always a big threat. Your product could become redundant over time, so thinking ahead, foreseeing potential issues and having a plan to future-proof your business is absolutely critical.

If your company's profitability drops (either suddenly or over a relatively short period of time) as a result of a market event or externality, it can significantly affect your business's valuation (which is directly linked to profitability and the number of customers/subscribers in most cases). When valuations change, it may affect your capacity to borrow, and banks loans can be called in, impacting dramatically on businesses that are supported by those borrowings.

It's always of great importance to have an emergency plan for running the business under changed conditions, and for how you would quickly restructure to meet those changed market conditions. You will need to be clear in your own mind about which staff are critical to retain, ensuring sales continue to be supported as much as possible, what work you and your core staff can possibly cover and what services could be temporarily outsourced while maintaining the core operating function.

Re-budgeting and re-planning in detail is essential at this point in time. To ensure you don't run out of cash, spend time with your accountant and go over and over the numbers until you're both confident that the business is recoverable and sustainable. Then you need to re-work the plan to grow the business from this new base and the new market conditions to once again ensure long-term sustainable success and the opportunity to exit.

If you need to wind things up

For some, new market conditions will undermine the viability of the business and there will be no option but to make the call to close the business. If this is the case, it needs to be done quickly and cleanly with all liabilities met while you have the cash available to meet them. Sit down with your accountant and calculate all staff entitlements and company liabilities, including suppliers to be paid and customers to collect money from. Then map out a process for closing down, informing staff and liquidating assets.

Again, if things are done quickly and properly you have a chance of getting back on your feet and preserving assets and your reputation. No-one will blame you for having a go. It's a fact that, unfortunately, market conditions change. If suppliers and customers have been managed professionally and all debts settled, then you're good to try again. If you go down in a burning mess, taking suppliers' money, the bank's money and business partners with you, it becomes so much harder to recover your reputation and start again at a later time, and financially it will take so much longer to recover.

Managing externalities

Insurances play a key role in managing externalities and surviving unpredictable events. For example:

- 'key person' insurance: in the event of your death or illness (or that of a business partner)

- professional indemnity insurance: protection if you're providing professional advice

- product insurance (product faults)

- public liability insurance.

Most insurance companies these days offer a business package where these key insurances can be bundled together at an affordable price and tailored to suit your business.

If the externality affects the entire market, the way you react, pivot and re-define your business and take advantage of the new market conditions may enable you to suddenly emerge as the new market leader. Those businesses that successfully use these situations to their advantage are the ones that have most likely already thought through the scenario and are prepared.

The bottom line is (yes, I'll say it again): if you run out of cash it's 'game over'... so make every effort to keep your business efficient and adaptable, and plan for externalities.

Essentially...

- React quickly to market changes to preserve capital.
- Plan for the unexpected and be prepared.
- Those who can adapt quickly to new market conditions can emerge as the new market leader.
- Ensure you have the right insurances in place.
- Don't let your business run out of cash!

CHAPTER 16

Managing growth and consistency

There's no easy stage when running a business. The challenges just change and there are some quite significant milestones that can introduce these changes.

As we've seen, in the early stages of a business the challenges are around validating your business model and understanding that there's a customer willing to pay the price for your product or service. It's about raising enough cash to start trading and getting early pilot customers to test your product and service levels and give quality feedback so you can keep refining the model, getting ready for prime time and preparing for rapid growth.

This book is about providing you with the fundamental elements you need to consider to ensure you have the best chance of success. Many people can't be bothered putting in the hard yards to validate their business model, and sitting down with their accountant to constantly run over the numbers and the 'what if' scenarios to understand exactly how much they need to sell and at what price and profit margin. Then there's determining who the customer is, and how they'll communicate with them and determine whether they will buy the product or service. Unfortunately, many will jump two feet in on a hunch without doing the groundwork and research first, and as a result simply waste a lot of money spoiling their chances of success. This will also often ruin their confidence or their financial opportunity to try again, even if they do things the right way the next time.

Once you get to the key $1 million revenue point and you've successfully navigated the initial challenges of getting your business validated and established, a whole lot of other challenges suddenly enter the equation:

- Managing inventory (optimal stock and re-order levels).

- Managing customers and collecting money.

- Managing supplier relationships and logistics costs.

- Managing people, payroll, tax liabilities and holiday leave.

- Managing cash flow, the bank and investors.

- Governance (creating a board or advisory board).

And the list goes on.

Systemising your business for growth

The only way to successfully grow a business rapidly is by building systems, processes and procedures—like a user manual on how your business will operate—and then delegating authority to key people to run those systems. The business can't simply revolve around you and grow, because if you need to control everything you'll become the bottleneck to growth. This is where the fundamentals of quality management come into play.

When my brother Greg and I were building the Regency Food Services business, we found our staff were constantly coming to us with virtually every issue they had to deal with, asking us what we wanted to do. There was always someone at my door with a problem. It made it impossible to get any of my own work done, which was critical to developing the business. As tends to be the case in any early-stage business, you want to help your staff and make sure everything is done correctly even though this doesn't end up helping you or the business and creates a culture where the staff place all the responsibility back on you and the problems just keep coming.

One of the things we learned early on in business was almost forced upon us. Hazard and critical control point (HACCP) analysis legislation was being introduced into the food distribution industry to identify any points of possible contamination and to control potential hazards. We wanted to position ourselves as leaders in the industry and to be the first to be prepared for this new legislation, which drove us to being one of the first companies in Australia to undertake the ISO 9001 quality management certification process.

For a relatively small company, this was a hugely time-consuming process and forced us to write detailed job descriptions for all our employees that cross-referenced every key task they were responsible for to the associated processes and procedures. These had to be written in detail that dealt with everything from how we took orders, including how we answered phones and how we spoke to people, through to the confirmation and processing of orders, how the warehouse and stock was managed, how orders were picked, how trucks were loaded, how deliveries were made... everything! It was a daunting task.

As young, first-time business owners, what we discovered during this arduous process was that something magical was starting to happen. I was suddenly in a position where I could tell those who were lining up outside my office to refer to their procedure for how to manage an event or a scenario and gave them the authority to manage it. Initially I would ask them to suggest how they should manage it, then I would ask them to make the decisions and report the results and eventually I would only need to know if something went wrong and needed my attention. If a new scenario occurred that the procedures didn't currently deal with, we would document it and build it in so that next time we knew how to manage that issue and it was no longer a problem. This is the process of continual improvement and corrective action. Quite quickly the line of people and constant interruptions stopped, and my brother and I had time to work on the business and continue to innovate and apply our ideas, moving the business ahead in leaps and bounds.

Different levels of delegation authority are also a great way to manage pay levels within your business and can be used in creating your organisation chart, linking delegation authority to positions or levels on the chart, or directly to position descriptions. If people don't want to accept responsibility, it limits their ability to progress within the business. This starts to focus you back on the recruitment process because you want to be hiring people who can grow and be promoted within the organisation and take on different levels of responsibility. People who can eventually become part of your senior management team.

Having a structure and framework made us realise we had fundamentally systemised our business and created a platform that could cope with rapid growth. Without it we would continue to flounder and be faced with ongoing barriers to growth. This was a vital lesson that I was able to apply to ZEN Energy right from the very early days, and when the market was ready to launch with unprecedented demand, the business was ready and able to grow with it, with consistency in its operation so customers' expectations were always met and, in most cases, surpassed. ZEN had a three-year average annual growth rate of over 400 per cent, which we simply could not have managed without an internal quality management system and a leading-edge accounting platform, on which we made sure we used every feature possible to improve our service offering.

If you asked me what is the number one key to success, it would be *consistency*. This comes through adherence to structured processes and procedures so everyone who interacts with your business gets a consistent experience day in, day out. A great experience every time is fantastic, and will definitely lead to satisfied customers making great reviews and referrals. Paradoxically, consistently poor service isn't necessarily bad if what your customer is after is a cheap price and they receive it each time. That's probably the consistency they're after and they simply accept the poor service that comes with it. When your performance is good one day and bad the next, that's the fastest way to lose customers and receive terrible reviews. People don't like inconsistency, and people delivering the service are often the worst culprits, so rigorous training in the business culture, values and how your staff are to interact with all your stakeholders is essential. And when I say your stakeholders', I mean everyone from your customers to your suppliers to your staff to finance providers and anyone else key to your business. Then it's information: people like to be well informed on a regular and timely basis that's consistent every time and has no surprises.

The 'crystal ball' plan for the future

An incredibly valuable exercise for entrepreneurs entering the scale-up phase is to imagine your company in five years time and at 10 times its current revenue. What would it look like and how would you get there? Start-ups and even scale-ups are so lost in their busy day-to-day world that they find it extremely difficult to imagine themselves and their company into the future, but it's a vital part of planning.

Start with the end goal in revenue and profit and step back year by year looking at every key aspect of your business, from the infrastructure you need, to the organisation chart of people and positions, the inventory and logistics and the marketing and sales processes. Once you have a systemised approach to your business, you'll be surprised how the scaling plan can fall into place and suddenly you can see the five-year pathway and how it could become real.

Then come back to year one, where you have the most clarity, and fill in the detailed goals of what needs to be achieved. Take your staff on the journey so everyone is aligned with the plan and buckle up for a rocket ride!

Mentors and peers

Finding an appropriate mentor or, even better, a support network of people who are experiencing similar challenges and willing to share their experiences is an invaluable learning platform.

Back in 1998, after Regency Food Services had won South Australian Entrepreneur of the Year, we caught the attention of the Young Entrepreneurs' Organization (YEO), a global networking and development group for business founders. It had originated in North America a few years prior and was just starting to establish itself in Australia. They were setting up 'chapters' in each state and were looking for someone to establish and become the founding president for South Australia—and I was the perfect fit at the time.

I agreed to establish the chapter and brought together a group of the state's brightest young entrepreneurs, all completely passionate about their purpose and all absorbed by their businesses. The qualifying criteria at the time was being under 40 years of age and the founder, co-founder or controlling shareholder of a business with a revenue in excess of USD$1 million.

It was a group designed purely to share experiences both from within the businesses and personally. From my own personal situation, none of my friends back then even owned a business, let alone a large business. They didn't understand the hours I worked and thought I was mad! The opportunity to bring a group of like-minded, 'half crazy' people together was one of the most formative times within my business career and I'm proud to say that many of the early members of EO (as it is now known) are among my closest lifetime friends.

As members were starting to reach 40 years of age, everyone was having such a great time they decided to change the name globally to the Entrepreneurs' Organization (EO) and took away the age limit. I maintained my membership for 20 years until 2019 and proudly saw out the incredible 20th anniversary celebrations, taking the group back on a journey over the 20-year history and the many adventures and stories we shared together over that time. The opportunity to talk through and share experiences in a structured format on how both you and other members navigated all the different challenges in managing a business is absolutely invaluable. A topic is put on the table by the presenter for the night and each forum member shares their personal experience in how they dealt with that particular scenario.

This also helps you keep up to date with industry trends, legalities, the latest technology people are using, how they are recruiting and retaining people, how they are controlling their cash flow and the experience of managing all their stakeholders including bankers, investors, customers and suppliers.

Beyond my own companies, the EO experience allowed me to be a close witness to the commercialisation and growth of two to 300 companies during that time, opening my eyes to the inherent traits of successful entrepreneurs.

Of those, one of the most powerful traits is the ability to focus intensely. It's a trait of genius and a curse at the same time. It's so important to try and maintain a life balance and slow down the pace a little to make time to look after yourself and those around you. As entrepreneurs we are so focused on building the future that we forget about the here and now. We get completely absorbed by our businesses, and we often forget to take the blinkers off occasionally and smell the roses.

Growing at the speed of SWEAT

SWEAT's experience saw them move quickly from dealing with tens, to hundreds, to hundreds of thousands of people literally within a matter of months and it wasn't even a full technology-enabled business at that point (just an eBook and website). Tobi classed it more as an e-commerce business at the time. It wasn't until a few years later that they started

(continued)

---

writing legitimate software applications and became multi-platform with supporting software engineering and product teams.

They had to focus on being more sustainable and building capability, which was an ongoing educational process and realisation as they evolved. A level of discipline was applied to everything as the company grew to maintain consistency of operation, from marketing campaigns to creative content development to fitness content development. They felt like they exhausted the things they could tidy up and create efficiencies within, particularly harnessing technology. Their photoshoots, for example, went from costing $300 to $500 000 per shoot in some cases, and then pulling it back to just tens of thousands once structures and outcomes were well defined. Tobi describes their efficiency improvement over time as 'insane' relative to how well they were able to run the business.

That discipline, however, didn't seem to carry over into their financial planning and analysis, as it's one thing to understand growth and revenue gain, another to read a P&L statement, and yet another to harness that information and strategically analyse financial information and plan for the long term. Tobi didn't start to develop these skills until about 12 to 18 months before they exited the business via their sale to iFIT. At that point, he says, 'the ship is already moving' and the trajectory is largely pre-determined in preparing the business for a potential acquisition opportunity.

Flavia on rapid growth

Flavia says, 'I face growth knowing that I am moving from 30 people to 100, yet some companies move from 100 to 1000'. In just four years, Fleet Space has gone from two people to 100 people, which is good but not massive in Flavia's view. She feels this is just a small percentage of the massive growth that's about to come. 'It's about how we move from 100 to 1000 in the next couple of years.' She still sees the company as small when she considers SpaceX now has 10 000 people ... it's just a step.

Flavia has a very clear vision of what her company will look like at various stages of future growth, including employee numbers and what infrastructure and systems will need to be in place. As you move from 20 to 30 employees and then from 50 to 500, at every stage of growth you remove 'hats' from people, allowing them the freedom to actually do their job.

Flavia relates this to her own position as a founder wearing 50 hats, then 40 and now 20:

> At every stage I can get better at my job. Having 50 hats is really hard. You can only give the bare minimum to each job, but as you remove hats you can achieve so much more, and it becomes so much more exciting.

Many people see growth as painful. However, Flavia sees growth as 'amazing!'

> Growth is maintaining consistency in two separate areas: operations and culture. When you grow, people try to overcomplicate things, which is dangerous for innovation and creativity. You don't want a million procedures and processes that slow down or stop progress, so ideally you want to keep the structure simple. You must be very careful as to what stage in your growth you allow more complicated structures to come into play; otherwise it will stall innovation.

Flavia admits this balance can be really hard to achieve. She is a strong believer in work-life balance and will not sacrifice her mental health, working 9 am to 5 pm or sometimes 6 am to 3 pm, but strictly controls her working hours. As a result, she packs a lot into her day to get the most out of the time she is working.

Simon on growth at Haigh's

Haigh's growth has been relatively consistent and controlled, opening about two stores per year. Haigh's now has strong systems and training programs in place to ensure consistency in both its retail and manufacturing operations. Some of these are in the process of being

(continued)

updated or have already been updated to cope with the new ways the business had to adapt and operate throughout the COVID-19 pandemic. For example, the simple and long-appreciated act of handing out samples in store had to be adjusted to meet the new hygiene standards.

Many retail systems had to change during the pandemic, particularly in training. Simon says, 'Zoom works well, but it's not the same as face-to-face training on the floor as you don't pick up the subtleties of human interaction'. The pandemic years certainly provided challenges to implementing training programs, with the focus more on keeping the stores open and being able to continue trading. Even system upgrades in line with their internal IT roadmap to assist in managing growth were delayed or had to be put on hold during the pandemic due to the lack of regular IT support and resources to manage the upgrades.

Training is also an issue for Haigh's when launching into a new geographic area; if you only have one store in a region, there is no training store for retail staff. This is always an issue for the first store in a region. Once you open a second store, one store can become a training store for the other. Then, of course, there is the additional manufacturing demand and ensuring transport logistics are in place that can cope with the temperature requirements of moving packaged chocolates across the country.

Essentially...

- Once you progress your business beyond start-up and into scale-up, you start to face the real challenges of running a fast-growth business and this is where most businesses fail, due to lack of experience.

- To prepare for rapid growth you must stop doing everything and start the process of systemising your business. This includes the creation of processes, procedures and job descriptions with delegated authority and a process for continual improvement.

- Consistency is the key to a successful business. The 'systemising' of your business, together with rigid training and role-playing, will enable a consistent approach to all facets of your business.

- Cast your mind into the future and produce a five-year plan that shows a 10 times growth in revenue and work back year by year including the detail of what needs to be put in place to make it happen. The most detail needs to be shown in year one.

- Find a mentor and/or join a business network where you can share your experiences and learn from others.

- Take time for yourself and those closest to you.

CHAPTER 17

Getting out of business

When starting a business, you must have a plan to get out of the business and maximise the business's value in the process. This is where some of the principles we've discussed in the book start to come together.

As your number of customers, revenue and profits increase over time, you're building value in your business, and at some point both you and your investors are going to want to realise that value. If investors are investing an amount of money today, they generally don't want that money sitting there forever. They will want to understand how you're going to add value to the business and then how they can exit the business at the increased value in a few years' time (usually a three- to five-year horizon) and make a significant profit. (Remember the investor pitch (presentation) described in chapter 11.)

Knowing who the target acquirers of your business are and how you'll make yourself enough of a nuisance to get their attention is key from the start. Disrupting and changing the way an industry operates is the ideal way of gaining the attention of large players in your industry. They will need to adapt their business if they are going to compete—which, if they are an old, established business and brand, could cost them an extraordinary amount of money. It may also take too long to change the existing culture and business model, and it may simply be more cost effective to buy the new upcoming business and brand and integrate into or extend their existing business and eliminate a problem opposition at the same time.

As mature businesses develop over time and the early founders and innovators exit, it often becomes harder for a business to maintain its entrepreneurial capability, particularly as new shareholders become more risk averse over time. Depending on the culture of the business and the risk tolerance of new shareholders, they may have a mandate to continually invest in research and development, but many will look for new up-and-coming businesses and technologies they can invest in to take their primary business forward faster and maintain their competitiveness. They will have generally built up a strong balance sheet (asset backing or 'war chest') over time and when the time is right, they will go on the hunt.

If your business is performing well and making good returns, you may be happy to keep it moving along and not sell. There's nothing wrong with this, although if you're doing well, you'll most likely get tempting offers along the way so all shareholders will need to stay well aligned and have a clear strategic plan. You also don't want to miss the boat if you don't realise the market is slowly turning and you've left your best days of value creation behind — and then can't get out of business later if you decide you want to. Many people have made the mistake of holding on too long.

So, the trick is positioning yourself in the market to attract the right offer and then picking the right time to sell to maximise your company's value.

With Regency Food Services it was a multinational that was entering the country and saw our business model as the one they wanted to replicate across Australia. We knew they really wanted the business as they had already made about three offers during the year, all of which we had refused. Eventually they made an offer we couldn't refuse, and my brother and I agreed we had maximised the value we could contribute personally and achieved the right price for the business — so we sold it.

Techniques for positioning your business for sale can be in the form of selling your product or service to the target company. Demonstrate the value you provide to them, and the market advantage they have gained and how that is sustainable over time. Make your business critical to their business; keep innovating and evolving so they can see a forward development pathway, but at all times protect your intellectual property via patents and trademarks so it can't be stolen.

Alternatively, the positioning could be achieved by stealing key contracts and accounts from your target business with new innovative ways of doing business, an enhanced product offering or a service that they can't compete with.

Whichever way you choose, you must outline the strategy to investors and incorporate the smart use of PR to build a profile, which will be crucial in the process so that potential acquirers get to read about you, your company, your brand and the market success you're enjoying.

Apart from target competitors, investors also seek to read about successful growing businesses and their strategies, so this third-party validation of your business through PR will often attract more investors if you want to continue to fund growth and build for a larger planned exit in the future.

The SWEAT exit

Even when an agreement has been made, the buying party will always find some risk with the business when carrying out their due diligence. They will use this information to either discount the price or will want warranties or indemnities against this risk to protect themselves from any future related costs. The threat or concern is that the buying party may walk away from the deal if these conditions aren't satisfied, which is what happened to SWEAT in 2019.

The more information the potential purchaser asks for and the more information you give them, the more grounds are available for negotiation. It can be a vicious cycle. Tobi naturally met this with a high degree of anxiety and didn't want a repeat of the 2019 deal when SWEAT entered negotiations with iFIT in 2021 during the COVID-19 pandemic.

(continued)

Negotiations can drag on for long periods, testing your fortitude, making you question yourself and your business, and creating deal fatigue. You can easily be distracted and take your eye off the business; the numbers slip as a result and then this of course finds its way into the negotiation. In terms of the business' human assets, Kayla was the front person and most important talent — and a gigantic marketing asset for the organisation — whereas Tobi ran the day-to-day business as an executive. As such, he experienced how the emotional weight of the negotiation process can be physically exhausting.

SWEAT completed the deal with iFIT in July 2021, selling for a reported $400 million. The company had an annual revenue of $100 million reaching a global community of more than 50 million women across its social media channels to help them reach their fitness goals. The app is translated into eight different languages and available in 155 countries. iFit would have seen plenty of opportunity for them to continue to add value to the business under their platform, enhance their overeall offering and also eliminate a key competitor at the same time.

Tobi has recently set up a new business, undertaking mentoring and advisory work, and is a shareholder and investor in a few other companies not related to fitness and health. He is keeping himself quite free, with his eyes always open and looking for more opportunities. He is looking at what's happening in the world and where he wants to go next, starting from a very different position: 'I'm working to a different level now. My main goal is to build something large that contributes to society'.

What does the future hold for Fleet Space?

Fleet Space will be mass manufacturing its own satellites in a new facility by the Adelaide airport that the federal government has provided $66 million towards. Each of the satellites will be entirely 3D printed (very cool!) and something that no-one in the world has done before, which will be a massive achievement and pretty amazing!

Fleet Space intends to build 50 satellites a year (all 3D printed) and reach $60 million to $80 million annual revenue over the first five years, along with building a steady road map towards a potential public listing (IPO), unless a large company with the necessary resources buys them out beforehand — but Flavia sees this as unlikely due to Fleet's size and value.

Flavia concedes some companies have gone down the path of listing pre-revenue to raise funds but sees this as 'super high risk' because everything is unproven and very theoretical, whereas Fleet Space has now proven its technology and business model and is very well positioned moving forward.

The future for Haigh's

The immediate future for Haigh's is a focus on the Queensland expansion of its retail division. This brings a focus back on the expansion of manufacturing to keep up supply to the new region and is core business for Haigh's. Simon says,

> It's always chicken and egg for us: if the retail stores return to full capacity, then we will have a manufacturing constraint and need to expand manufacturing rapidly. If they don't, then we'll have excess manufacturing capacity to support the retail expansion.

As we saw earlier, Haigh's has now secured land for the expansion of its manufacturing so it's ready to go either way.

What's not core business is logistics and the challenges with new states and warehouses, so consideration is being given to potentially outsource this part of the business. Other companies are geared up to do this better and this would free up capital to fund the expansion of both the retail and manufacturing divisions of the Haigh's business at a faster pace.

The appointment of an independent board to manage Haigh's strategy and transition to the next generation on behalf of the family is a significant but secure and sensible step in the company's business and in staying true to its history and planning for the future.

Essentially...

- Start planning your exit from the very beginning so that it's part of your validation focus and long-term strategy.

- Being disruptive (changing the way a business or sector operates) is a great way to get noticed and become an acquisition target.

- Look for ways to integrate your business with target acquirers.

- Use smart PR as third-party validation and endorsement to attract acquirers or more investors.

ARE ENTREPRENEURS BORN OR MADE?

The age-old question of what makes a successful entrepreneur has long been debated. Are there any common traits that they are potentially born with? How much is instilled from the environment they are raised in? How much is learned?

Successful entrepreneurs have the unique ability to be able to focus intently and not be distracted from achieving their goals. They always find ways to get past obstacles that would stop most people in their tracks, and they manage to re-invent industries and themselves. I see these skills as a combination of three key elements:

1. *Tenacity* to not let go of your passion.

2. *Creativity* to think laterally and to see things differently, to piece together things others have missed.

3. *Resilience* to get back up and continue to find a way and not give up at the first obstacles put in front of you — to not accept 'no, that can't be done' for an answer when you know it can be done.

So let's look at the question, 'What might successful entrepreneurs be born with?' Firstly, it's the ability to focus intently and lock everything else out. Examples of world-class entrepreneurs who are well recognised for being 'on the spectrum' include Bill Gates, Elon Musk and Mark Zuckerberg. They sometimes appear socially awkward yet have an innate intelligence and focus that sets them apart with the depth of their thinking.

This can be a social disadvantage, and potentially detrimental to their families in the longer term if not controlled. However, it can also be an advantage in creating complex strategic plans and technologies that can block competitors and disrupt industries: like thinking 10 moves ahead in a game of chess, a deeper understanding of where the world is heading and the needs of consumers in the future. So, I see this as a trait in successful entrepreneurs, though as much as the world needs these remarkable, insightful people, it is often much to their own personal detriment. They are often not the brilliant academic minds at school—and quite often the opposite, even the troublemakers at times. They just see things differently.

Tobi's thoughts...

Tobi believes that, like many things in life, you must be open to it, and he agrees there are traits you're born with and there's a lot to learn. It's not necessarily about being open to entrepreneurship. Tobi thinks that's too generic, as the definition of entrepreneurship is simply to move money from one area to another to generate a high return.

In modern society, if you removed most things and left yourself with discipline and curiosity, they are really the foundational traits you need. Being disciplined to get stuff done and curious enough to be open to learning. While Tobi agrees that some people are inherently born that way, he also believes it's false to say you need those things to be successful as they are also quite subjective.

He says there is a huge portion of people that are 'born an entrepreneur' in the natural way, but then there's a whole bunch of people who by 'nature and nurture' through others, or through their environment, become entrepreneurs because it becomes a need. Tobi liked the idea and wanted to be an entrepreneur, but it wasn't until the opportunity presented itself that he got to go down that path and test his ability.

The second point about the question, 'What might successful entrepreneurs be born with?' is about how much is instilled in them from their upbringing. I feel this is a more neutral point as I see plenty of successful entrepreneurs who were brought up in business families, were taught how to run a business and experienced all that goes with it from an early age and want to do the same. This is where the mentors are inside the family and the learnings and culture are developed from an early age. There's an old saying that the first generation starts a business, the second grows it and the third (who have never experienced the hard work that goes into starting and growing a business) is often the one to bring it down. So the generational instilment of 'work ethic versus entitlement' is an area worthy of further study.

On the other hand, I have also seen entrepreneurs who have come from difficult backgrounds—who just want a better life for themselves and their families—and have a great idea. These are people (often immigrants) who have the tenacity and resilience, and through sheer determination have found mentors, educated themselves, got backers, found customers and learned how to get started. It's often the person who isn't bound by education and rules, the one who sees things differently, who is the disrupter. Sara Blakely is an incredible entrepreneur who went from stand-up comedian to selling fax machines door to door, to having a great idea that would revolutionise women's undergarments, and through sheer determination with a disruptive product found her first backers and built the billion-dollar Spanx empire!

So, on this point, I see people from all upbringings who have become successful entrepreneurs, which brings me to the third point: 'What can be taught and learned?' Everything covered in this book is 'learning'. There is no such thing as common sense—just shared experience, and with entrepreneurship there's a point where natural ability and education cross over and education takes over.

Understanding how to validate a business idea—who is the customer, how to reach them, how to carry through with your business values and rules of engagement to make sales, how to protect your IP, how to set up consistent systems to enable growth, how to present to stakeholders and investors and how to position your business for an eventual exit—are all vital lessons that can make or break a business.

These are not things that anyone just knows. For me, learning about entrepreneurship and seeking mentorship from people who have created successful enterprises previously is where it all comes together. This can enable anyone with the right tenacity, creativity and resilience to build a great business.

Flavia's thoughts...

Flavia says, 'Funny thing is, up to 30 years of age I didn't know what an entrepreneur was!' No-one she knew, even within her family, was an entrepreneur. She had no idea how a start-up worked and admits she 'kind of didn't want to do it'.

She loves space and is a self-confessed nerd, a scientist, who had never started anything. It just happened to her... 'the more you go, the more you need to learn as you go'. Flavia is now doing a directorship course.

'You need to be madly in love and passionate about something to be an entrepreneur and succeed,' she says. And she just loves what she does!

I hope the principles covered in this book all make coherent sense, bring some order into how you create and grow your business and becomes part of your shared experience, which you can then share with those around you so that we all have the chance to make our ideas come to life.

Don't forget to stay in touch on the companion website for book updates, stories, templates and calculators: www.essentialentrepreneur.com

We all learn from each other's stories about how we have dealt with some of the topics in this book and the issues raised. Please share your stories with us and we will share the best and most relevant examples with the Essential Entrepreneur community. There's a tab on the website page called 'Stories' where you can upload your story as well as read other stories that our followers have shared with us that could provide valuable insights and experience.

These stories will form the content for great conversations for the Essential Entrepreneur podcast channel, which you can link to from the companion website.

Wishing you all the best with your entrepreneurial adventures!

Richard Turner
The Essential Entrepreneur

ACKNOWLEDGEMENTS

There are a number of people who have contributed to the writing and creating of this book who I am indebted to and I would like to gratefully acknowledge their support. All of these people have a passion for supporting start-ups and scaling businesses and I can't recommend them and their companies' services highly enough:

- Madderns — trademark and patent attorneys
  Bill McFarlane — Senior Partner, Madderns
  (madderns.com.au/team/bill-mcfarlane)

- Motus Legal
  Craig Yeung — Director and Founder, Motus Legal
  (motuslegal.com.au/our-team)

- i2 Advisory — chartered accountants
  Kevin Johnson — Senior Partner, i2 Advisory
  (i2advisory.com.au/team/kevin-johnson)

- Metric Marketing
  Laura Turner — Operations Manager, Metric Marketing
  (metric.com.au)

- Peter Fisher Photography
  Peter Fisher — Director and Founder, Peter Fisher Photography
  (peterfisher.net)

INDEX

account terms 79–80

accounting course, doing 13

adaptability to markets 149–150

Adwords 53

after-sales-service, customers' experience of 70–71

ahead of the game, being 86–89

Alibaba 75

aligning to customers 83–85

amounts to raise 106, 112

anchoring in pricing 64

'angel investors' 99

anti-dilution clauses 116–118

Artesian Alternative Investments, Kirsten Bernhardt's role in *xvii–xviii*

Artesian Venture Partners (AVP) 104

assets 19–20

assigning shareholdings 112–114

Australian Investment Council 120

author, childhood and start in business *x–xii*

authority, delegation of 158

bait and switch tactic 64

balance sheets 14–15, 16–17, 19–20

Balcrest Stud 10

batching orders 67–68

Bernhardt, Kirsten
— introduction *xvii–xviii*
— on investors and VCs 103–108

Blakely, Sarah and Spanx 175

'bootstrapping' 98

brand
— designing 127–128
— evolution of SWEAT as 58–59

brand (*continued*)
—importance to Fleet Space
Technologies 59
—positioning 49–50
—protection with
TMs 125–131
brands 49–52
business
—getting out of 167–171
—setting up your 24
business architecture stack
40–42
business model
—keeping simple 142–145
—validation of 105–106
business plan, developing a
start-up 11–26

campaigns, designing 56
capital to raise 106, 112
cash-flow statements
14–15, 18–19, 21
communication, importance
of 70
companion website,
author's 118, 176
consistency as key to success
158–159
cost validation 14–21
critical business matters and
minority shareholders 115
'cross-docking' 80
'crystal ball' planning 159
culture creation 42–43
current assets and liabilities 20

customers
—after-sales-service experience
of 70–71
—aligning to 83–85
—difficult 71
—learning from the experience
of 71
—testing out 54–56
customs, foreign 77

defective products 77–78
delegation of authority 158
deposits, charging 66
design, importance to Fleet Space
Technologies 59
difficult customers 71
dispatching stock 68
'down rounds' 117
drag-along rights 118
drop-shipping warehouses
66, 80–81
'dumb money' 99

'elevator pitches' 99
engagement of staff 44
entitlement vs work ethic 175
entrepreneurs, successful 173
Entrepreneurs' Organization
(EO) 160–161
equity 20
Espacenet 133
executing the plan
—Flavia Tata Nardini on 26
—Tobi Pearce on 25
exit strategy, having an 107

'experience', retail shopping
    as an 69
externalities, managing
    152–153

'first user rights' 127
Flavia *see* Tata Nardini, Flavia
Fleet Space Technologies *see also*
    Tata Nardini, Flavia
—executing the plan 26
—founding of *xiv–xvi*
—funding journey of 122
—future of 170–171
—importance of brand and
    design to 57
—patents to serve customer
    needs 138
—perfect timing for 35
—validating the business 6–7
flexible model of shareholding
    113
focused, staying 141–142
foreign customs 77
formal assignment of
    shareholdings 113–114
founders, advice to 107–108
'founding teams' 104
freight forwarding 79
funding
—amounts to raise 106
—methods of 21–22
future, planning for 159

game, being ahead of 86–89
Garnaut, Professor Ross 87, 89

Georges department store,
    Sydney launch 36
GFG Alliance 87–88
go-to-market plan 13–14
going wrong, things 70–71
Google patents 133
Greensmith Energy
    Management 87
grid-scale energy storage 87
growth, systemising business
    for 156

Haigh, Simon, introduction
    xvi–xvii
Haigh's Chocolates
—and chocolate cafés 148
—experience with patents 138
—future of 171
—good and bad timing
    for 36–37
—growth at 163–164
—history of *xvi–xvii*
—market research by 60–61
—passion and culture over
    generations 46–47
—self-funding by 122
—start-up story 8–10
—third-generation innovation
    by 90–91
—validating the business 9–10
hazard and critical control point
    (HACCP) analysis 157
HeadStart process 130
home solar energy 32–33
house brand in pricing 65

innovation
—by Haigh's 90–91
—Flavia Tata Nardini on 89
insurances 152
intellectual property (IP)
    rights 132
international sourcing 75–81
inventors, identifying 134
investors, finding 98–99
ISO 9001 quality management
    certification 157
Itsines, Kayla *xiii*

landscape searches 133
lateral thinking 85–86
learning for entrepreneurs
    175–176
learning from customers'
    experience 71
leavers, good vs bad 118–119
leaving a business 167–171
liabilities 20
limited partners (LPs) 103
local sourcing 74–75
logistics provider, choosing 68
logos, designing 127–128
loss leaders 64
low energy homes, building 144

market, researching your 52–53
market adaptability 149–150
market categories, new 93–94
market conditions, rapid changes
    in 150–151

market enquiries, converting to
    sales 63–64
market timing 33
market traction and 'Series A'
    companies 105, 106
market validation 12
marketing 52–58
marketing campaigns,
    designing 56
marketing cycle 57
mentors, finding 23, 160–161
minimum order quantities
    (MOQs) 78–79
minimum viable product
    (MVP) 97–98
minority shareholders
    having a say 115
motivation of staff 44

'national phase' applications
    136–137
new market categories 93–94
non-disclosure agreement
    (NDA) 2, 12
non-participating preferences 116

OKR (objectives and key results)
    methodology 43
operating models 13–14
options 119–121
orders, batching 67–68

participating preferences 116
passion, keeping alive 42–43

Patent Cooperation Treaty (PCT)
— applications 135–136
— filing 136–137
patents
— analysing search results 134
— completing 135–136
— lodging provisional 134–135
— for novel innovations 132–137
— searching for 133
Pearce, Tobi *see also* SWEAT
— executing the plan 25
— introduction *xiii–xiv*
— start-up story 2–5
— on traits of entre-
preneurs 174
Pearson, Matt *xiv–xvi*
peers, finding 160–161
performance assessment using OKR 43
phone answering 65
phone calls, value of 70
picking lists 68
pitching your idea 99–102
'positive cash flow' businesses 66
pre-payment 66
'pre-seed' money 98
predatory pricing 65
preference shares 115–116
price discrimination 65
price skimming 65
pricing
— predatory 65
— subscription 65–66

— techniques of 64–66
'prior art' 134
priority dates for patents 134–135
product vs service 27–28
products, Haigh's market research on 60–61
profit and revenue 12–13
profit-and-loss statement 14–16
profitability 21
'prosecution' phase of patents 137
provisional patents, lodging 134–135, 137
public relations (PR), engaging help with 57–58

quality management certification (ISO 9001) 157

raising capital 106, 112
Regency Food Services
— as 24-hour food distribution service 83–84
— naming of 50
— selling 168
— systemising the business 156–157
— and total foodservice 32
— and value in business 143
Regency Staffing 50, 85–86
registered designs, rights over 131
reporting clauses 119
retail shopping as an 'experience' 69
revenue and profit 12–13

sales, converting market enquiries
    into 63–64
satellites, 3D printed 170–171
scale-up stage
    — criticality of 102
    — entering 159
search engine optimisation
    (SEO) 53
'seed rounds' 102
'seed stage' companies 105
selling a business 168
'Series A' companies 105
service response 67–71
service vs product 27–28
setting up a business 24
shareholder agreements 114–121
shareholdings
    — assigning 112–114
    — unequal 114–115
shipping times and delays 80
shopping centres, Haigh's
    thoughts on 60–61
simple, keeping business
    model 142–145
Sinek, Simon, TED Talk video 55
'smart money' 99
sourcing
    — international 75–81
    — local 74–75
South Australian Venture Capital
    Fund (SAVCF) 107
Spencer, Raymond 86–87
staff, hiring and firing 149–150
start-up grants 22
start-up stage 97–102

start-up story
    — Flavia Tata Nardini 5–8
    — Haigh's Chocolates 8–10
    — Tobi Pearce 2–5
stock, dispatching 68
store locations, Haigh's market
    research on 60–61
'strip shopping', Haigh's
    move into 61
subscription pricing 65–66
successful entrepreneurs, key
    elements of 173
support networks, finding
    160–161
SWEAT *see also* Pearce, Tobi
    — equity in 121
    — evolution as brand 58–59
    — executing the plan 25
    — founding of *xiii–xiv*
    — importance of timing
        for 34–35
    — passion, culture and values
        of 43–45
    — productisation of service 29
    — rapid growth of 161–162
    — selling the business 169–170
    — validating the business 4–5
    — video production
        by 145–146
'sweat shops' 73
systemising business for
    growth 156–158

tag-along rights 118
taglines, designing 127–128

Tata Nardini, Flavia *see also* Fleet
    Space Technologies
— executing the plan 26
— focus of 148
— on innovation 89
— introduction *xiv–xvi*
— passion, culture and
    values 45–46
— on rapid growth 162–163
— start-up story 5–8
— thoughts on
    entrepreneurship 176
thinking laterally 85–86
3-year forecast 22–23
3D printed satellites 170–171
timing 31–37
'total foodservice' 32
trademark attorneys, consulting
    128–131
trademark registration, applying
    for 126–127
trademarks (TMs) 125–131
truck fleet, owning and operating
    143–144
24-hour food service
    distribution 84

upbringing of entrepreneurs 175
'use of funds' 106

valuation, not getting
    hung up on 108
value in business 143
venture capital (VC) market
    overview 103–108
video production by SWEAT
    145–146

warranties 77–78
warrants 119–121
website, companion 118, 176
'weighted average cost
    method' 117
winding up a business 151–152
work ethic vs entitlement 175
wrong, when things go 70–71

Young Entrepreneurs'
    Organization (YEO)
    160

ZEN Energy
— as brand 126
— early business architecture
    stack 41
— timing of 32–33
— transition to 50–51
ZEN Home Energy Systems
    33, 40, 50–51, 93–94